P9-CAD-371

Frommer's®
Portable
Turks & Caicos
4th Edition

by Alexis Lipsitz Flippin

WILEY

John Wiley & Sons, Inc.

Published by:
JOHN WILEY & SONS, INC.
111 River St.
Hoboken, NJ 07030-5774

ISBN 978-1-118-28822-1 (paper); ISBN 978-1-118-33490-4 (ebk);
ISBN 978-1-118-33155-2 (ebk); ISBN 978-1-118-33378-5 (ebk)

Editor: Andrea Kahn
Production Editor: Heather Wilcox
Cartographer: Guy Ruggiero
Photo Editor: Richard Fox
Production by Wiley Indianapolis Composition Services

Front cover photo: Iron-shore beach on Providenciales, Turks and Caicos Islands.
©SuperStock / AGE Fotostock, Inc.

For information on our other products and services or to obtain technical support,
please contact our Customer Care Department within the U.S. at 877/762-2974,
outside the U.S. at 317/572-3993 or fax 317/572-4002.

Wiley also publishes its books in a variety of electronic formats. Some content that
appears in print may not be available in electronic formats.

Manufactured in the United States of America

5 4 3 2

CONTENTS

LIST OF MAPS

ABOUT THE AUTHOR

A former Frommer's Senior Editor, **Alexis Lipsitz Flippin** is the author of *Frommer's St. Martin, St. Barts & Anguilla* and *Frommer's New York City with Kids* and a coauthor of *Frommer's Caribbean* and *Frommer's 500 Extraordinary Islands*. She has written and edited for numerous consumer magazines and websites, including *Self, American Health,* CNN.com, Weather.com, and *Rolling Stone.*

HOW TO CONTACT US

In researching this book, we discovered many wonderful places—hotels, restaurants, shops, and more. We're sure you'll find others. Please tell us about them, so we can share the information with your fellow travelers in upcoming editions. If you were disappointed with a recommendation, we'd love to know that, too. Please write to:

Frommer's Portable Turks & Caicos, 4th Edition
John Wiley & Sons, Inc. • 111 River St. • Hoboken, NJ 07030-5774

ADVISORY & DISCLAIMER

Travel information can change quickly and unexpectedly, and we strongly advise you to confirm important details locally before traveling, including information on visas, health and safety, traffic and transport, accommodations, shopping, and eating out. We also encourage you to stay alert while traveling and to remain aware of your surroundings. Avoid civil disturbances, and keep a close eye on cameras, purses, wallets, and other valuables.

While we have endeavored to ensure that the information contained within this guide is accurate and up-to-date at the time of publication, we make no representations or warranties with respect to the accuracy or completeness of the contents of this work and specifically disclaim all warranties, including without limitation warranties of fitness for a particular purpose. We accept no responsibility or liability for any inaccuracy or errors or omissions, or for any inconvenience, loss, damage, costs, or expenses of any nature whatsoever incurred or suffered by anyone as a result of any advice or information contained in this guide.

The inclusion of a company, organization, or website in this guide as a service provider and/or potential source of further information does not mean that we endorse them or the information they provide. Be aware that information provided through some websites may be unreliable and can change without notice. Neither the publisher nor author shall be liable for any damages arising herefrom.

FROMMER'S STAR RATINGS, ICONS & ABBREVIATIONS

Every hotel, restaurant, and attraction listing in this guide has been ranked for quality, value, service, amenities, and special features using a **star-rating system.** In country, state, and regional guides, we also rate towns and regions to help you narrow down your choices and budget your time accordingly. Hotels and restaurants are rated on a scale of zero (recommended) to three stars (exceptional). Attractions, shopping, nightlife, towns, and regions are rated according to the following scale: zero stars (recommended), one star (highly recommended), two stars (very highly recommended), and three stars (must-see).

In addition to the star-rating system, we also use **seven feature icons** that point you to the great deals, in-the-know advice, and unique experiences that separate travelers from tourists. Throughout the book, look for:

🎁 **Special finds**—those places only insiders know about

💬 **Fun facts**—details that make travelers more informed and their trips more fun

☺ **Kids**—Best bets for kids and advice for the whole family

📷 **Special moments**—those experiences that memories are made of

✋ **Overrated**—Places or experiences not worth your time or money

✍ **Insider tips**—great ways to save time and money

🏷 **Great values**—where to get the best deals

The following abbreviations are used for credit cards:

AE American Express	DISC Discover	V Visa
DC Diners Club	MC MasterCard	

TRAVEL RESOURCES AT FROMMERS.COM

Frommer's travel resources don't end with this guide. Frommer's website, **www.frommers.com**, has travel information on more than 4,000 destinations. We update features regularly, giving you access to the most current trip-planning information and the best airfare, lodging, and car-rental bargains. You can also listen to podcasts, connect with other Frommers.com members through our active-reader forums, share your travel photos, read blogs from guidebook editors and fellow travelers, and much more.

THE BEST OF THE TURKS & CAICOS ISLANDS

The Turks and Caicos Islands (TCI) are a coral-reef paradise. Even with the advent of real tourist development and the bustle of construction—particularly on the main island of Providenciales (nicknamed Provo)—the beauty and tranquillity of this island chain remain intact. What has put Turks and Caicos on the map is its wealth of gorgeous beaches—360km (224 miles) of them, to be precise—and the magnificent underwater life just off its shores.

Beaches The 19km-long (12-mile) **Grace Bay Beach** (p. 15) is Provo's most luscious stretch of sand. From Provo, you can take a beach excursion to the island's offshore cays, the **Caicos Cays,** to find pristine sand dollars. On **Middle Caicos,** green cliffs tower over the sparkling sapphire seas of **Mudjin Harbor** (p. 20), and casuarina pines fringe the pillowy sands of **Bambarra Beach** (p. 20).

Things to Do Scuba divers explore the **Wall** (p. 89), off **Grand Turk,** where the island's western edge plunges 2,134m (7,000 ft.) into the deep. For world-class bonefishing, head to the saltwater flats of **Middle Caicos** to hunt the elusive "ghost" of the sea. Swim alongside humpback whales in **Salt Cay.** Visit **Little Water Cay** (p. 26), a nature preserve for indigenous rock iguanas.

Eating & Drinking You will dine very well in Provo on dishes from around the world, but if it's local flavor you're craving, head to Provo's **Blue Hills** (p. 53), where casual beach shacks serve such regional favorites as peas 'n' rice, curry fish, johnnycakes, and conch.

Da Conch Shack (p. 43) serves up fresh conch fritters, conch stew, and conch chowder.

Nightlife & Entertainment   The party vibe on Provo is easygoing and laid-back. For prime sunset viewing, the Grace Bay Club's beachfront **Lounge** (p. 64) has a glowing fire pit, and the **Infinity Bar** (p. 64) is a sleek ribbon of black marble inset with sexy blue lights. Enjoy ripsaw music at the **Wednesday and Sunday barbecues** at the **Osprey Beach Hotel** (p. 101) in Grand Turk.

THE best BEACHES

Enveloped by the world's third-largest coral reef, the Turks and Caicos Islands are home to some of the finest powdery-sand beaches and most stunning turquoise seas in the world. Most are just minutes away from an airport, and you'll rarely have to vie for beach space with anyone else. Tour operators can whisk you to uninhabited cays where you can play Robinson Crusoe for a day. The waters are pristine and diamond-clear, and waves rarely rise above a gentle ripple—perfect for kids and snorkelers of all ages.

o **Grace Bay Beach** (Providenciales): This 19km (12-mile) stretch of pale sands and azure seas is the pride of Provo; Grace Bay Beach was named the World's Leading Beach for several years running at the World Travel Awards. An increasing number of resorts and condo hotels have sprung up along the shore. Like much of the TCI, the beach is fringed by a coral reef system with fabulous snorkeling and diving. See chapter 2.

o **Malcolm Beach** (Providenciales): The traditional way to see this charming cove (often referred to as Malcolm Roads Beach) is with a 4×4 along twisting, bumpy Malcolm Roads. You can also access the beach by staying at Amanyara (the resort is adjacent to the beach) or by getting a tour-boat operator to take you there. Its waters are part of the Northwest Point Marine National Park. See chapter 2.

o **Long Bay Beach** (Providenciales): The calm, shallow waters of this quiet beach on Provo's southeastern shore make it perfect for young children. Take a horseback ride on the beach here with Provo Ponies. See chapter 2.

o **Sapodilla Bay & Taylor Bay** (Providenciales): Part of the Chalk Sound National Park, these shallow bays along Provo's southwest coastline have soft, silty bottoms and stunning blue water. See chapter 2.

o **Pine Cay** (Caicos Cays): The money shot in many a photo spread of the Caribbean islands is this private island's perfect crescent of sand, ringed by azure seas. It's the front yard of the Meridian Club resort. See chapters 2 and 4.

- **Parrot Cay** (Caicos Cays): Another gorgeous private island, Parrot Cay has a lovely stretch of sugary sand graced by beach bums of the celebrity variety. See chapters 2 and 4.
- **Three Mary Cays** (North Caicos): Up until now, only boaters and those in the know found their way to this spectacular snorkeling beach. See chapter 2.
- **Whitby Beaches** (North Caicos): The coves of **Three Mary Cays** are prime snorkeling spots. Step into the shallows of the palm-fringed **Pelican Point Beach** (in front of Pelican Beach Hotel) and find conch shells of every size. Lovely **Horsestable Beach** has enjoyed its North Caicos seclusion for years (it's also a prime bird-watching spot). See chapter 2.
- **Mudjin Harbor** (Middle Caicos): This beach is as stunning seen from the green cliffs towering above as it is up close. You can explore the turquoise shallows and look for colored beach glass on the sand ringing Dragon Cay. See chapter 2.
- **Bambarra Beach** (Middle Caicos): Casuarina trees fringe this picturesque, unspoiled beach. Its shallow aquamarine waters stretch into the horizon and are the site of the festive Valentine's Day model sailboat races. The Middle Caicos Day beach party is held here in August. See chapter 2.
- **Governor's Beach** (Grand Turk): Grand Turk's most celebrated beach is a nice spot for a swim and a picnic under shady pines. It's in the Columbus Landfall National Park—more about Columbus's "landfall" later—and within sightlines of the Grand Turk Cruise Center, which welcomes mammoth cruise ships 4 to 6 days a week. See chapter 5.
- **Pillory Beach** (Grand Turk): The Bohio Dive Resort is set on the prettiest beach in Grand Turk, just right for swimming. See chapter 5.
- **The Beaches of Salt Cay:** This tiny island has some beautiful stretches of sand, and excellent snorkeling just offshore. Yours will be the only footsteps in the sand along 4km (2½-mile) North Beach. See chapter 5.

THE best OUTDOOR ADVENTURES

The waters here are superlative for all kinds of outdoor adventures, from diving and snorkeling to sailing, kayaking, and fishing. But watersports aren't the only game in town. You'll find prime golf and tennis facilities in Provo—and Rollerblade hockey is all the rage with local school kids. See chapters 2 and 5 for more on outdoor sports.

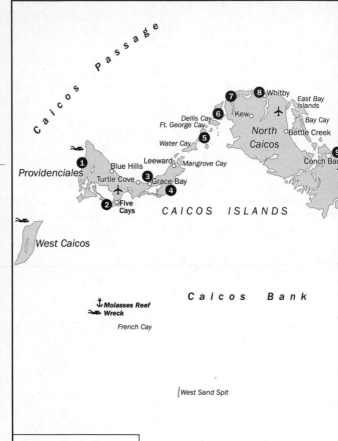

Bambarra Beach **10**
The Beaches of Salt Cay **13**
Governor's Beach **12**
Grace Bay Beach **3**
Long Bay Beach **4**
Malcolm Beach **1**
Mudjin Harbor **9**
Parrot Cay **6**
Pillory Beach **11**
Pine Cay **5**
Sapodilla Bay & Taylor Bay **2**
Three Mary Cays **7**
Whitby Beaches **8**

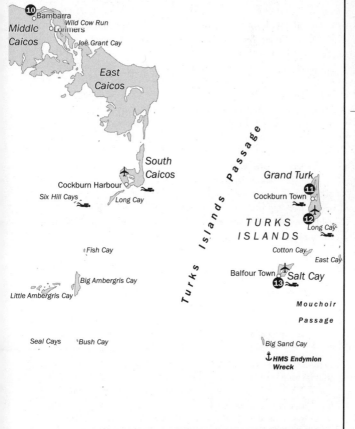

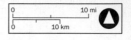

ATLANTIC

OCEAN

10 Bambarra
Wild Cow Run
Middle ○Lorimers
Caicos
Joe Grant Cay

East
Caicos

South
Caicos

Cockburn Harbour ○
Six Hill Cays
Long Cay

Fish Cay

Big Ambergris Cay
Little Ambergris Cay

Seal Cays   *Bush Cay*

Grand Turk
Cockburn Town **11**

12
Long Cay

TURKS
ISLANDS
Cotton Cay
East Cay

Balfour Town **13** *Salt Cay*

Mouchoir
Passage

Big Sand Cay
⚓ *HMS Endymion*
Wreck

T u r k s   I s l a n d s   P a s s a g e

o **Snorkeling the Islands:** The snorkeling opportunities are excellent throughout the islands, and you should take the time if you have it to explore the Caicos Cays, North Caicos, Middle Caicos, South Caicos, Grand Turk, or Salt Cay. But you don't even have to leave Grace Bay to find good snorkeling: The government has established snorkel trails at Smith's Reef (just outside Turtle Cove) and Bight Reef (in front of the Coral Gardens resort). These reefs are right off the shoreline, providing easy access to a fragile but beautiful world. See chapter 2.

o **Taking a Beach Cruise** (Caicos Cays): A number of tour-boat operators offer variations on half- and full-day beach sojourns. Your trip may include a stop on **Little Water Cay,** a protected nature reserve inhabited by a colony of rare rock iguanas; snorkeling the coral reefs and diving for conch; or combing the beaches of uninhabited cays for sand dollars and other shells. See the "Caicos Watersports Operators: Master List" box on p. 22.

o **Fishing the Elusive Bonefish** (Middle Caicos): The vast, hushed Lorimer flats off Middle Caicos are prime bonefishing territory; you'll need an airboat to get where even the locals have never been. See chapter 2.

o **Strolling Grace Bay Before Sunset:** You'll be surprised at the long stretches of beautiful beach you have all to yourself. The sand is a little cooler, and the water takes on the pink and purple hues of the setting sun. Stop in and sink into an inviting white-cushioned perch at the **Lounge** (p. 64) or the **Infinity Bar** (p. 64), the oceanfront bars at the Grace Bay Club, and sip a cocktail while you wait for the green flash on the horizon during sunset (seeing it is said to bring good luck). See chapter 2.

o **Watching the Glowworms Glow:** Four or 5 days after a full moon, millions of glowworms come out just after sunset to mate—lighting up the shallow waters with a sparkling green glow. Take a glowworm cruise in the Caicos Cays or off any number of Caicos Bank docks. The show is over when the mating ritual ends and the female glowworms devour the males. See chapter 2.

o **Hiking or Biking the Crossing Place Trail** (Middle Caicos): This old coastal road, first established in the late 1700s by settlers and slaves working the local plantations, has been reopened from the Conch Bar to the Indian Cave field-road section and is now a National Trust heritage site. It has heartbreakingly beautiful sections, some on bluffs overlooking the blue-green ocean shallows and rocky outcrops; others bordered by island brush that includes wild sea-island cotton, remnants of the 18th-century plantations, and elegant sisal plants. Follow hiking or biking trails; when you get hot, take a swim in the shallow coves below. Be sure to visit

Conch Bar Cave, a massive aboveground limestone cave system used by Lucayan Indians some 600 years ago. See chapter 2.

o **Diving the Wall off Grand Turk:** You can find great scuba-diving spots throughout the TCI, including spectacular opportunities off Provo's Northwest Point and in West Caicos. But Grand Turk's electrifying dives are just some 274m (900 ft.) offshore, where the continental shelf drops off from the coral reef in dramatic fashion. Along the ledges of this sheer wall is marine life in all its eye-popping plumage. See p. 89.

o **Whale-Watching on Salt Cay:** From January through April, humpback whales migrate along the 2,134m (7,000-ft.) trench of the Columbus Passage (which snakes between the Turks islands and the Caicos islands) on their way to the Silver Banks to mate and calf. You can actually snorkel and swim alongside these gentle 15m (50-ft.) creatures. See chapter 5.

o **Finding Treasures on the Beach:** The currents drop off a good amount of flotsam and jetsam on these windward TCI beaches—much of it worthless junk. But hey, one man's trash is another man's inspiration. Nearly every island has a visionary artist or two who dabbles in beach salvage. Of course, real treasures do wash up: In 2006, silver pieces of eight and an 18th-century spyglass were picked up on the Salt Cay beaches. And bottles containing messages have found their way here from all over the world; the Turks & Caicos National Museum has a sprinkling of messages in a bottle. The water's edge also yields gorgeous shells, from snow-white sand dollars to queen conch shells—but remember: Always return a shell to the sea if something is living inside. See chapter 5.

THE best LUXURY RESORTS

Most of the country's accommodations are on Providenciales, where condo hotels are the prevailing lodging option.

o **Amanyara,** Northwest Point, Provo (© **866/941-8133**): The Singapore-based Amanresorts' first foray into the West Indies deftly marries pampered luxury with an exacting Eastern aesthetic; the name means "peaceful place." Guest pavilions are utterly private and smartly appointed in Aman teakwood, polished terrazzo floors, and state-of-the-art toys for grownups. See p. 79.

o **The Gansevoort,** Grace Bay, Provo (© **888/844-5986**): Urban escapees are making a beeline for this great-looking Lower Bight property; it's definitely in their comfort zone. It's got a happening pool scene, a sizzling bar, and ultrastylish rooms with irresistible touches, like electric blinds, big freestanding tubs (filled from a ceiling tap), and glass-encased rain showers. See p. 69.

- **Grace Bay Club,** Grace Bay, Provo (© **800/946-5757**): This Grace Bay pioneer continues to reinvent itself, and everything, from the spacious luxury suites to the unparalleled service, is first-rate. Don't expect attitude, however; this is one of the warmest, most welcoming spots in town. You can even have a private dinner served under the stars on the beach. See p. 60.

- **Point Grace,** Grace Bay, Provo (© **888/209-5582**): Set on a stunning crescent of Grace Bay beachfront, this resort gets consistent high marks for its handsomely appointed British-Colonial–style suites and ultraromantic restaurant, Grace's Cottage. See p. 64.

- **The Regent Palms,** Grace Bay, Provo (© **866/877-7256**): There are no bad rooms at this gorgeous resort, with a serpentine infinity pool, shops, restaurants, and a 2,300-sq.-m (25,000-sq.-ft.) spa with reflecting pools. It offers both serenity and a lively nightlife, with the Plunge Bar heating up at sunset. See p. 65.

- **The Somerset,** Grace Bay, Provo (© **877/887-5722**): Size matters, and this Tuscan-style boutique resort is just small enough to have a personalized, intimate feel and just big enough to offer sprawling luxury suites with monumental balconies and marble-clad kitchens and baths. It has a sunny, serene atmosphere and a beautifully landscaped pool and beachfront. The house restaurant, O'Soleil, is one of Provo's best. See p. 66.

- **The Veranda,** Grace Bay, Provo (© **877/945-5757**): It looks like Main Street by the Sea, more like a movie-set village than an upscale resort: houses with gingerbread trim, picket fences, wooden porches, and broad swathes of neatly trimmed green. See p. 67.

- **West Bay Club,** Grace Bay, Provo (© **866/607-4156**): This boutique oceanfront property has 46 spacious, beautifully appointed suites with full kitchens and marble-clad bathrooms. But unlike its neighbor the Gansevoort, West Bay has no sizzling pool scene or hipster vibe. Here it's all about those spacious rooms and that beachfront location and a warm and welcoming hands-on management that makes you feel as if you're old pals. Call it mom-and-pop luxe. See p. 76.

- **Parrot Cay Resort,** Parrot Cay, Provo (© **866/388-0036**): Yes, this is the exclusive island resort where Ben Affleck married Jennifer Garner and Bruce Willis owns a home. But it's also a pretty wonderful place to unwind and de-stress, whether you're stretched out on the secluded beach or thrilling to a treatment by a Balinese masseuse at the world-class COMO Shambhala spa. See p. 81.

- **The Meridian Club,** Pine Cay, Provo (© **866/746-3229**): This is luxury of a determinedly understated, no-frills variety. You'll be without TVs, radios, even air-conditioning, but you'll want for little else on this secluded private island, which offers a kind of solitude and serenity found in few places in the world. The beach and watersports opportunities are superb. See p. 82.

THE best INNS & GUESTHOUSES

Inns and guesthouses are virtually nonexistent on Provo, but are often the main lodging on the outer islands. Personal service is a hallmark of these small inns and guesthouses.

o **Blue Horizon Resort,** Mudjin Harbor, Middle Caicos (© 649/ 946-6141): This small eco-resort is sitting pretty in a breathtaking setting on Middle Caicos, with a resident fishing expert and plenty of thrilling eco-activities on offer. New owners have freshened up the freestanding cottages with crisp linens and a sunny palette. You'll enjoy unbelievably scenic views from your cottage perch. Add a gorgeous beach below, and the sense of having a stretch of paradise largely to yourself—what more could you ask for? See p. 84.

o **Grand Turk Inn,** Front Street, Grand Turk (©/fax 649/946-2827): The big, comfortable suites are laid-back luxury personified. The innkeeper is a hospitality pro, and the 150-year-old restored Methodist manse is Grand Turk's best accommodation. The sweeping Atlantic panorama from the upstairs sundeck is simply awesome. See p. 100.

o **Island House,** Lighthouse Road, Grand Turk (© 649/946-1519): This small inn enjoys a quiet perch on a Grand Turk hill, with views over the island's sloping green bluffs. Rooms are nicely renovated, and the freshwater pool is set in a lovely courtyard framed in tropical blooms. You aren't on the beach, but you're not far, and the inn provides vehicles to get you there and back. See p. 100.

o **Manta House,** Duke Street, Grand Turk (© 649/946-1111): These three large, handsomely renovated suites enjoy a prime spot on Duke Street. Run by the same pair of sunny Aussie sisters who operate the Sandbar across the street, the Manta House is island comfort personified. See p. 101.

THE best MODERATELY PRICED LODGINGS

Let's face it: Although you can find affordable lodgings on the other islands, bargain hotel rooms in Provo are few and far between. Save on hotel rates by taking advantage of the special packages advertised on most hotel websites, and consider traveling in the off season, when rates are deeply discounted. Also consider villa rentals (see chapter 6 for more information). Here are my choices for the best of the islands' less-expensive accommodations.

o **Sibonné Beach Hotel,** Grace Bay, Provo (© **800/528-1905**): A stay here means a room just steps away from the waters of Grace Bay for a steal. Charming Sibonné is one of the oldest resorts on Grace Bay, and its rooms—all of which have sea views, by the way—are nothin' fancy but nicely appointed. But the real steal is the oceanfront apartment with full kitchen and two patios— one screened and one open, each with the same meltingly lovely view of Grace Bay that many of its pricier neighbors share. See p. 78.

o **Caribbean Paradise Inn,** Grace Bay, Provo (© **649/231-5020**): The owner, Jean Luc Bohic, has fashioned a comfy little B&B around a tropical courtyard and pool, a 2-minute stroll from Grace Bay. The gourmet restaurant Coyaba brings in a lively scene at night. See p. 77.

o **Comfort Suites,** Grace Bay, Provo (© **888/678-3483**): This is a perfectly decent place to stay; the pool area is attractive, and the suites are spacious. And the location is prime: 1 block from Grace Bay and next door to the Ports of Call shops. See p. 77.

o **Pelican Beach Hotel,** Pelican Beach, North Caicos (© **877/774-5486**): The price is right at this modest spot smack-dab on Pelican Point. Rooms are nothing special, but the beach is quite nice—and the food, cooked by owner Susie Gardiner, is superb home-style island fare. See p. 83.

o **Bohio Dive Resort,** Front Street, Grand Turk (© **649/946-2135**): Set in a prime location on beautiful Pillory Beach, this hotel has rebuilt after Hurricane Ike, and its rooms (the suites have kitchenettes) are spacious and clean; ask about the reasonable dive/lodging packages. Bohio has a sensational restaurant/bar and a beach bar. See p. 99.

THE best **FAMILY RESORTS**

The TCI is as much a first-rate family destination as it is a top honeymoon retreat. Plenty of properties offer ways to entertain and pamper the kids. Here are my top choices for great family fun.

o **Beaches Turks & Caicos,** Lower Bight Road, Provo (© **800/232-2437**): Beaches keeps walking away with top honors as one of the region's top family resorts. And why not? It's got *Sesame Street* characters ambling around the property, camps and daily activities, kid-targeted restaurants, and a full-service nursery. And somehow the landscaping is immaculate. See p. 68.

- **Grace Bay Club,** Grace Bay, Provo (© 800/946-5757): The setup here couldn't be better for accommodating both families and romantic twosomes—each has its own set of villas, pools, and restaurants. The resort's Kids Town has a clubhouse with daily activities and "campouts" on the beach. See p. 60.

- **Ocean Club Resorts,** Grace Bay, Provo (© 800/457-8787): It's family fun all the time at these popular resorts, with day camps, great pools, and kitchens. See p. 74.

- **Royal West Indies,** Grace Bay, Provo (© 800/332-4203): This sprawling resort is another spot that deftly accommodates both families and couples, with full kitchen facilities and a kiddie pool set apart from the "Quiet Zone" pool. It's got a terrific casual restaurant that somehow satisfies both grownups and little ones. See p. 75.

- **The Sands at Grace Bay,** Grace Bay, Provo (© 877/777-2637): This has always been one of the top spots in Provo for families (fully equipped kitchens, nice pool, great beach), and with a major makeover and refurbishment, it's better than ever. It even has a giant toy box in the sands of Grace Bay crammed with beach toys. See p. 75.

- **Seven Stars,** Grace Bay, Provo (© 866/570-7777): With a big kids' playground and lockout capacity for two- and three-bedroom suites, this resort is tailor-made for families. It's got the only heated pool on the island (saltwater, too!), a nice touch for little ones learning to swim. See p. 70.

- **The Somerset,** Grace Bay, Provo (© 877/887-5722): Its sprawling suites are tailor-made for families, as is the infinity pool. Add to that a kid-friendly Caribbean staff that gets to know the little ones on a first-name basis, a big enticement for families to come back year after year. See p. 66.

- **West Bay Club,** Grace Bay, Provo (© 866/607-4156): The nicely appointed suites have full kitchens, roomy bathrooms, and enormous closet space. The pool has a tiered section for toddlers, and the hands-on management couldn't be more hospitable. See p. 76.

THE best RESTAURANTS

You will eat very well on these islands, whether dining on fresh conch in an outdoor beach shack or sampling a chef's multicourse tasting menu in an elegant five-star resort. Here are some top picks.

- **Anacaona,** Grace Bay, Provo (© 649/946-5050): The setting for the Grace Bay Club's premier restaurant is unbeatable: You're seated under the stars, surrounded by flaming torches, on a tiered and lushly planted landing overlooking Grace Bay Beach. The food is as dreamy as the ambience. See p. 47.

o **Bay Bistro,** Sibonné Beach Hotel, Grace Bay, Provo (© 649/946-5396): It's one of the most pleasing spots to dine in Provo—set in a whitewashed wooden open-air porch above Grace Bay Beach. Now you can sit closer to the beach on outdoor decks in the flickering light of tiki torches. The food is good and good value for Grace Bay. See p. 50.

o **Caicos Cafe,** Grace Bay Road, Provo (© 649/946-5278): New owners, a new chef, and a revamped, Mediterranean-style menu have proved a winning combination in this beguiling spot. It's not on the beach but it's charming nonetheless, set on the wooden deck of a gingerbread cottage. See p. 50.

o **Coco Bistro,** Grace Bay, Provo (© 649/946-5369): Most everyone who eats here comes away happy. The romantic setting in a garden of palms makes it a special-occasion place. The food makes it a must-occasion place. Stuart Gray is the hands-on owner/chef—you'll see him hollering out food orders as the glitterati swoop in. See p. 47.

o **Da Conch Shack,** Blue Hills, Provo (© 649/946-8877): Like many of its compadres, Da Conch Shack is scenically set above the Blue Hills beach. It's a popular spot, with good, fresh food (conch prepared to order) and a barefoot vibe. See p. 43.

o **Guanahani,** Bohio Dive Resort, Grand Turk (© 649/946-2135): You won't find a better place to eat in Grand Turk, what with South African chef Jorika Mhende at the helm. Overlooking Pillory Beach, the space is both warm and elegant. Sample the fiery peri-peri chicken or the delicious shrimp creole. See p. 96.

o **Island Thyme,** Salt Cay (© 649/946-6977 or 649/242-0325): It's the beating heart of this sweet little island, and full of life and light and bonhomie, whether it's pizza night, bingo night or Lobster Mania Thursdays. The food is a revelation: from state-of-the-art conch chowder to Asian-inspired "jumping steak." See p. 109.

o **Magnolia Restaurant & Wine Bar,** Turtle Cove, Provo (© 649/941-5108): The view alone is worth the trek up the hill above Turtle Cove marina, but the food can stand on its own. Seared rare tuna is a house specialty. Have a drink and watch Grace Bay glitter. See p. 55.

o **Mango Reef,** Alexandra Resort, Grace Bay, Provo (© 649/946-8200): In its new beachside location at the Alexandra Resort, this comfortable, casual spot is one of those places where the food is so reliably good you'll reach for excuses to eat here. See p. 52.

- **Pat's Place,** Historic South District, Salt Cay (© **649/946-6919**): Pat taught school on Salt Cay for 28 years. She now serves home-style island cooking on a modest porch behind her home. You'll feel like Mom is behind the stove when she brings out family-style platters of fish fingers, barbecued chicken, fried plantains, and rice 'n' peas. See p. 109.

EXPLORING PROVIDEN- CIALES & THE CAICOS ISLANDS

Most of the country's celebrated sports and activities revolve around, unsurprisingly, its ubiquitous resource: all that crystal-clear water with the mesmerizing sapphire hue. Try scuba diving the steep underwater walls just offshore, fishing the coral reef or deepwater drop-offs, or leisurely exploring the uninhabited cays and coves that dot the watery landscape.

Of course, the TCI has plenty of activities beyond watersports, including golf, tennis, horseback riding, exploring historical attractions, caving, shopping, and enjoying state-of-the-art spa treatments. This chapter tells you how to experience the best the Caicos islands have to offer.

BEACHES

It's no hype: The beaches of the Turks and Caicos are some of the most breathtaking on the planet, thanks in large part to one of the world's few remaining unspoiled coral reef ecosystems. This, the third-largest coral reef system in the world, helps act as a breakwater against ocean surges for these islands, keeping the coastal waters calm and clear. It makes its presence known on land as well: Coral is literally the soft white sand beneath your feet.

The Caicos islands have some of the country's best beaches, including world-class Grace Bay—and on many of them, yours will be the only footprints you'll see.

Note: All TCI beaches are public, and even the most developed residential beaches are required to have public access points. Make use of these access routes; never cross private property to get to a beach.

Providenciales

Grace Bay Beach ★★★   Starting at Leeward and running all the way to Thompson Cove, Grace Bay Beach is 19km (12 miles) of spectacular, powdery-soft white sand lapped by gin-clear, blue-green seas. Grace Bay has a smooth sand bottom (few rocks to speak of) and is generally tranquil and diamond-clear, making the beach ideal for young kids. You won't have the place all to yourself—resorts have rapidly developed along its edge—but Grace Bay is rarely crowded; in fact, if you walk far enough you'll discover many quiet, unpeopled stretches. Though Grace Bay has no public facilities, the resorts themselves come in handy; almost all have ocean-side cafes and bars with restrooms. Smith's Reef, near the Turtle Cove Marina, and Bight Reef, directly in front of the Coral Gardens resort, are two good snorkeling spots right on Grace Bay.

Grace Bay, Providenciales.

Long Bay Beach ★   Grace Bay Beach is so stunning that you might not want to venture anywhere else, but a few other beaches on the island are worth a look. In the east, Long Bay Beach lies on the shore opposite from Grace Bay, opening onto Long Bay itself. It begins around Juba Point, extending east to Stubbs Cove, and is virtually free of hotels (but is a growing residential area). The shallow waters are sheltered and have few waves, making it the perfect spot for young children. Take a horseback ride on the beach here with **Provo Ponies** (see "Horseback Riding on the Beach," below).

Long Bay, Providenciales.

Malcolm Beach ★★   If you really crave privacy, seek out Malcolm Beach. The traditional way to see this charming cove (often referred to as Malcolm Roads Beach) is by 4×4 along twisting, bumpy Malcolm Roads. You can also access the beach by staying at Amanyara (the resort is adjacent to the beach) or by getting a tour-boat operator to take you there. Its waters are part of the Northwest Point Marine National Park. There's good snorkeling, though you'll have to bring your own gear—unless, of course, you're a guest at Amanyara, which has excellent snorkeling and other watersports equipment. Be sure to lock valuables in the trunk of the car before you head to the beach.

West Providenciales.

Exploring Providenciales & the Caicos Islands

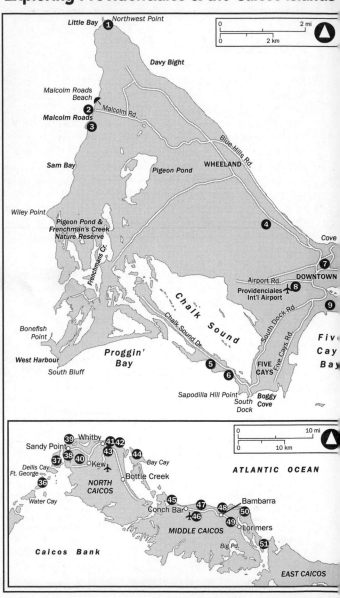

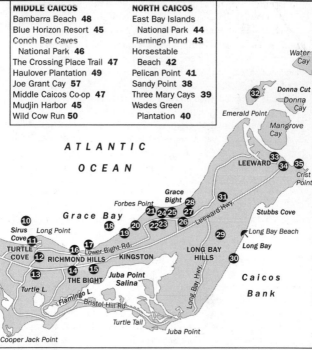

MIDDLE CAICOS
Bambarra Beach **48**
Blue Horizon Resort **45**
Conch Bar Caves
  National Park **46**
The Crossing Place Trail **47**
Haulover Plantation **49**
Joe Grant Cay **57**
Middle Caicos Co-op **47**
Mudjin Harbor **45**
Wild Cow Run **50**

NORTH CAICOS
East Bay Islands
  National Park **44**
Flamingo Pond **43**
Horsestable
  Beach **42**
Pelican Point **41**
Sandy Point **38**
Three Mary Cays **39**
Wades Green
  Plantation **40**

ATLANTIC

OCEAN

**PROVIDENCIALES
& THE CAICOS CAYS**
Amanyara **3**
Anani Spa **28**
Art Provo **24**
Athletic Club **15**
Beach Lounge at the
  Gansevoort **16**
Beaches Turks & Caicos
  Resort & Spa **19**
Bight Reef **18**
The Blue Hills **4**
Caicos Adventures **23**
Caicos Conch Farm **35**
Caicos Wear **26**
Casablanca Casino **27**
Cheshire Hall **9**
Club Sodax **13**
COMO Shambhala **37**
Danny Buoy's **22**
Dive Provo **26**

Exhale Spa **16**
Grace Bay Beach **17**
Heaving Down Rock
  Marina **34**
Infinity Bar **28**
Jai's **7, 25**
L'Raye Cinema **14**
Little Water Cay
  (Iguana Island) **32**
Long Bay Beach **30**
The Lounge at the
  Grace Bay Club **28**
Magnolia Restaurant &
  Wine Bar **12**
Maison Creole **8**
Malcolm Beach **2**
Northwest Point **1**
Parrot Cay **37**
Pine Cay **36**
The Plunge **20**
Ports of Call **26**

Provo Golf & Country
  Club **31**
Provo Ponies **29**
The Regent Spa at
  the Regent Palms **20**
Regent Village **25**
The Saltmills **15**
Sapodilla Bay **6**
Smith's Reef **10**
Taylor Bay **5**
The Thalasso Spa at
  Point Grace **21**
Turks & Caicos National
  Trust Shop **14**
Turtle Cove Marina **11**
Unicorn Bookstore **15**
Walkin' Marina/TCI
  Ferry Dock **33**

horseback riding **ON THE BEACH**

Long Bay Highway meanders up into the Long Bay Hills, home of **Provo Ponies,** off Dolphin Lane (www.provoponies.com; ✆ **649/241-6350** or 649/946-5252), which offers **horseback rides on the beach** ★★ for novices and seasoned riders alike. The Provo Ponies stables comprise a real menagerie, with friendly dogs roaming, roosters crowing, and 24 horses—technically big ponies—available to ride.

On our afternoon ride, we were assigned horses according to skill levels. As less-experienced riders, we were given a couple of old gentlemen whose days as Triple Crown threats are behind them. But even our gallant steeds picked up the pace when we hit the beach; the horses love the gentle sand, the cool breezes, and the open spaces. As do the riders: It's a relaxing, soul-satisfying experience.

Camille Slattery, the energetic owner of Provo Ponies, came to the Turks and Caicos 22 years ago to teach scuba diving and never left. Her stable grew along with her love of horses; she opened it to the public in 2002. Many of her horses are Grand Turk horses, which Camille calls "bomb-proof: so easy and so intelligent." A couple she even refers to as "babysitters"—they literally take care of the people riding them. These horses can take the heat because they're born and bred here; still, the stable doesn't schedule any midday rides, for the benefit of both horse and rider. Provo Ponies offers two rides a day along the secluded, untrammeled Long Bay Beach, in morning and late afternoon. Rides last an hour or 90 minutes, and helmets, fanny packs, and water are provided. Provo Ponies takes beginners or experts—and only allow cantering if the rider shows he or she is experienced. They also offer private swimming rides. What is it about riding a horse on a tropical beach? As Camille says, "It's everybody's fantasy." A 1-hour ride is $75; a 90-minute ride is $90 (hotel pickup/drop-off included). Rides are Monday through Saturday, 9:30am and 3:30pm in the winter, and 9:30am and 4:30pm in the summer (12 riders maximum per trip; maximum 200-lb. weight limit; children 5 and under must have previous riding experience). Reservations are required.

Chalk Sound ★★ This landlocked lagoon west of the hamlet of Five Cays is one of the prettiest sights in Provo. **Sapodilla Bay** and **Taylor Bay** are part of Chalk Sound National Park. These beautiful, shallow bays along Provo's southwest coastline have soft, silty bottoms and warm water the color of blue topaz. Sapodilla Bay lies between two 9m (30-ft.) cliffs at Gussy Cove, stretching all the way west to Ocean Point. This is such a well-protected beach—with fine sands and clear shallow water (even a hundred feet out)—that the locals often refer to it as "the children's beach."

Chalk Sound National Park, Providenciales.

Caicos Cays

You may find yourself beachcombing for sand dollars on one of the lovely uninhabited cays of the Caicos Cays on a beach excursion offered by an area watersports operator. Many of these cays are protected TCI national parkland; all have slivers of beautiful, fine-powder beaches. Among them: **Little Water Cay,** a nature reserve that is home to a population of native rock iguanas (see "A Visit to Iguana Island," later in this chapter), and **Fort George Cay,** a National Historic Site. The high-rent development of **Dellis Cay** as a Mandarin Oriental hotel was on hold at press time.

Pine Cay ★★★   The main beach of this 324-hectare (800-acre) private island is a perfect crescent of white sand, a marketer's dream. The beach fronts the **Meridian Club** resort (p. 82). The island is also home to a number of private homes.

Parrot Cay ★★★   This gorgeous private island is the home of the celebrated Parrot Cay resort, with a movie-star clientele and a world-class spa. The island was originally known as Pirate Cay.

North Caicos

Three Mary Cays ★★   Down a rough, overgrown dirt road and just east of Sandy Point are the sun-dappled blue coves of Three Mary Cays (named for its three distinctive rocks). This is a prime snorkeling spot, home to colorful fish, lobster, and the occasional barracuda. Three Mary Cays is not easy to find, so get specific directions before heading out (and consider getting there in a four-wheel-drive).

Sandy Point, North Caicos.

Whitby Beaches ★★   The beaches of this seaside village stretch for 11km (7 miles) along the island's northern coastline. Step into the shallows of the palm-fringed **Pelican Point beach** (in front of Pelican Beach Hotel) and find conch shells of every size. Lovely **Horsestable Beach** has enjoyed its North Caicos seclusion for years and is a prime bird-watching spot and picnic location.

Whitby, North Caicos.

East Bay Islands National Park ★★   To the east of North and the northwest of Middle, these two uninhabited islands have long, sunlit stretches of turquoise shallows, tangled mangrove stands, and Bahamian scrub. The park is home to native rock iguanas and whistling ducks. You can take excursions to East Bay Islands with **North Caicos Boats** or **Amphibious Adventures** (see info below).

East Bay Islands National Park, North Caicos.

Middle Caicos

Bambarra Beach ★★★ Travel along the old Conch Bar on bluffs above the shoreline until you reach Bambarra Beach, where tall casuarina pines fringe a gorgeous stretch of white sand. Shallow emerald waters stretch from the beach all the way to Pelican Cay. The name "Bambarra" is believed to have originated from the slave survivors of the shipwreck *Gambia*, the Bombarra people of Africa. Many Middle Caicos celebrations are held here, including the annual Valentine's Day Model Sailboat Regatta.

Bambarra Village, Middle Caicos.

Joe Grant Cay ★★★ Set between Middle Caicos and East Caicos, this uninhabited island is a castaway's dream. It has a sheltered harbor on the leeward side and a picturesque sweep of beach on the windward side. You can take an excursion to Joe Grant Cay with **Amphibious Adventures** (see info below) on a trip to **East Caicos,** which also has lovely beaches on its north and east coasts.

Joe Grant Cay, Middle Caicos.

Mudjin Harbor ★★★ The green cliffs overlooking the sea in **Mudjin Harbor** provide a dramatic departure from the flat scrublands of Provo. Down below, sparkling jade waters crash around Dragon Cay, a sharp-toothed hulk of weathered limestone known as iron shore. Look for colored sea glass on the sand.

Mudjin Harbor, Middle Caicos.

Wild Cow Run ★★★ Getting to this isolated, undeveloped beach on the island's northeastern coastline isn't easy; it's a 45-minute drive from Bambarra Beach down a long, rocky road past the crumbling ruins of colonial cotton plantations and little else. At the end of the road, it's a short walk through casuarina pines to this beautiful beach, which is dotted with shells and sandbars that make for great swimming. Be sure to carry the necessary provisions with you before you head out: first and foremost, cell phone, water, and sunscreen. And go now; a development is selling parcels of land along Middle's northeastern coast.

Nr. Haulover Point, Middle Caicos.

SCUBA DIVING & SNORKELING

Scuba Diving ★★

Dive experts, including the late Jacques Cousteau, have cited Providenciales as one of the 10 best sites in the world. Why is the diving so good around Provo and in the Turks and Caicos in general? There are a number of reasons: great visibility (often more than 30m/100 ft.), gentle seas, a barrier reef that runs the full length of Provo's 27km (17-mile) north coast, dramatic vertical underwater "walls" where the coral is big and healthy and marine life congregates, and a local commitment to protecting its natural assets—much of the coastal waters around Provo are protected national parkland, where fishing is not allowed. The water is warm and calm throughout much of the year. (For more about diving in Grand Turk and Salt Cay, see chapter 5.)

From the shore at Grace Bay, visitors can see where the sea breaks along 23km (14 miles) of barrier reef, the teeming undersea home to sea life that ranges from colorful schools of fish to barracuda to rotund grouper.

Around Provo and the Caicos islands, the popular diving spots include **Grace Bay, Northwest Point** (a 4.8km/3-mile strip of excellent dive sites with a vertical drop-off to 2,099m/6,888 ft.), **Pine Cay, West Caicos** (with miles of 1,829m/6,000-ft. vertical walls), and **French Cay** (more 1,829m/6,000-ft. vertical drop-offs). The latter two are great spots to see large pelagics such as reef sharks, sea turtles, stingrays, and dolphins. For extensive information about each of these sites, go to the very informative website of **Art Pickering's Provo Turtle Divers Ltd.,** Turtle Cove (www.provoturtledivers.com; ✆ **649/946-4232** or 800/833-1341 for reservations). It's the oldest dive operation in the islands.

Most dive operators rent scuba tanks, plus backpacks and weight belts (included in the dive cost). In general, a single-tank dive costs $75, a night dive goes for $85, and a morning two-tank dive is $129 to $136. Many offer technical diving and PADI training, with full instruction and resort courses. An open-water PADI referral course goes for around $425 and open-water PADI certification is $585.

Snorkeling ★★

The snorkeling is as good as it is on Provo and the Caicos islands for the same reasons that the diving is so fantastic (see above). This is a prime place to learn to snorkel: The waters are clean, clear,

CAICOS watersports OPERATORS: MASTER LIST

Watersports activities are the name of the game in the Turks and Caicos, and in most cases you'll be availing yourself of the capable expertise of local operators and boat charters to get out and play in the miles of sea. Much of the coral reef is protected national parkland, and the water is too shallow for powerboats and personal watercraft (jet skis); only captained boats are allowed in these protected waters. **Sun & Fun Sea Sports** (www.turksandcaicos.tc/sunandfun; ℂ **649/946-5724**) rents out motorboats and personal watercraft for use in designated areas.

Most "beach excursion" boat trips are half-day or daylong cruises on spacious power catamarans that offer a variety of activities, including snorkeling, shelling, beach barbecues, conch diving, and visits to Little Water Cay (aka "Iguana Island"), a nature reserve where a population of endangered native rock iguanas enjoys protected status (see "A Visit to Iguana Island," later in this chapter). Many of the tour operators running these excursions can pick you up right on the beach if you're staying at a Grace Bay resort.

The following is a master list of the top watersports and charterboat operators in Providenciales and the Caicos islands. Most include free pickup/drop-off from your hotel to the marina and back in the price of the excursions.

o **Amphibious Adventures** (http://amphibiousadventures.org; ℂ **649/232-2588**): Sailing trips and eco-tours of some of the TCI's wildest and most remote islands.

o **Art Pickering's Provo Turtle Divers** (www.provoturtledivers.com; ℂ **800/833-1341** in the U.S., or 649/946-4232): Provo's oldest dive shop offers scuba diving trips, instruction, and equipment rental, as well as snorkeling, fishing, and beach excursions.

o *Beluga* **Charter Sailing** (www.sailbeluga.com; ℂ **649/946-4396**): Captained charter sailing on a Polynesian catamaran; beach excursions.

o **Big Blue Unlimited** (www.bigblueunlimited.com; ℂ **649/946-5034**): Provo pioneer in eco-adventures offers kayaking, snorkeling, mountain biking, stand-up paddling, and North/Middle Caicos trips. Also offers technical and recreational scuba diving, instruction, and equipment rental, as well as private charters.

o **Caicos Adventures** (Regent Village; www.tcidiving.com; ℂ **649/941-3346**): Scuba diving, instruction, and equipment rental; snorkeling; and beach excursions.

o **Catch the Wave** (www.catchthewavecharters.mobi; ℂ **649/941-3047**): Bonefishing, bottom fishing, and deep-sea fishing; beach excursions; water-skiing; island cruises (including cave and bird-watching trips); private charters.

- **Dive Provo** (www.diveprovo.com; *©* **800/234-7768** in the U.S. or 649/946-5040): Technical and recreational scuba diving, instruction, and equipment rental; hotel/dive packages; snorkeling.
- **Grand Slam Fishing** (www.gsfishing.com; *©* **649/231-4420**): Big-game fishing charters in a 46-foot Hatteras, a 40-foot pursuit boat, or a saltwater flats boat.
- **Kenard Cruises** (www.kenardcruises.com; *©* **649/232-3866**): Luxury cruises with Captain Kenard in a 42-foot power catamaran leave from Turtle Cove Marina.
- **KiteProvo** (www.kiteprovo.com; *©* **649/242-2927**): Kiteboarding rentals and lessons with certified instructors.
- **North Caicos Boats** (www.northcaicosboats.com; *©* **649/232-4141** or 649/947-7470): Boatbuilder and captain Howard Gibbs offers bonefishing, fly-fishing, bottom-fishing, and night-fishing charters as well as snorkeling, shelling, or sightseeing eco-tours in Middle and North Caicos and nearby uninhabited islands.
- **Ocean Vibes** (www.oceanvibes.com; *©* **866/450-3483** or 649/331-1104): Scuba diving, instruction, and equipment rental; scuba and snorkeling charters; multiday packages.
- **Reef Peepers** (www.reefpeepers.com; *©* **877/258-7333** or 649/231-4961): Glass-bottom-boat excursions; snorkeling trips; sunset cruises; private charters. Leaves from Turtle Cove Marina.
- **Sail Provo** (www.sailprovo.com; *©* **649/946-4783**): Sailing cruises; snorkeling cruises; combination beach excursion cruises; sunset catamaran cruises; weddings.
- **Silver Deep** (www.silverdeep.com; *©* **649/946-5612**): Scuba diving; snorkeling; bonefishing, bottom fishing, fly-fishing, deep-sea fishing, night fishing, and shark fishing; beach excursions and barbecues; glowworm cruises; sunset cruises; island getaways; private charters.
- **Sun Charters** (www.suncharters.tc; *©* **649/231-0624**): Sailing excursions and beach cruises aboard the *Atabeyra;* pirate cruises; private charters; weddings.
- **Windsurfing Provo** (in front of the Ocean Club East resort; www.windsurfingprovo.tc; *©* **649/241-1687**): Kiteboarding and windsurfing lessons and rentals; stand-up paddleboarding; beach kayaking.

temperate, and gentle, and the marine life is for the most part rich and thriving.

A number of watersports operators offer snorkeling trips (or combination snorkeling/beach excursions) off Grace Bay or in and around the Caicos Cays, a short (30-min.) trip from the marina at **Heaving Down Rock Marina** or **Turtle Cove Marina** (see "Caicos Watersports Operators: Master List," above). **Caicos Adventures** takes you farther still, on 4.6m-wide (15-ft.) powered catamarans, to superb snorkeling spots in West Caicos and French Cay, both about an hour's boat ride from Leeward (www.caicos adventures.com; ✆ **649/941-3346**).

You can even find great snorkeling opportunities right on Grace Bay. While most resorts along Grace Bay offer complimentary snorkeling equipment with which you can happily tool around the clear shallows in front of your hotel, it's unlikely that you'll see anything other than the clear turquoise sea and a sprinkling of pink-tinged seashells known as sunrise tellins or sun-bleached coral. If you really want to see an active underwater marine garden, grab your snorkeling equipment and head down the beach to one of Grace Bay's two prime snorkeling spots, Smith's Reef and Bight Reef, both in the Princess Alexandra National Park, on Provo's northern coastline.

Smith's Reef, near Turtle Cove Marina, is a walk-in dive to a seascape of brain and fan corals, purple gorgonians, anemones, sea cucumbers, sergeant majors, green parrotfish, long-nosed trumpet fish, an occasional southern ray, and a visiting hawksbill turtle or two. Smith's Reef has underwater signs that describe the coral reef ecosystem and the diversity of life that thrives there. Snorkelers can learn about the various creatures camouflaged within the reef, the importance of sea-grass beds, and the ways that parrotfish contribute to the environment. The trail follows the perimeter of the reef starting inshore in about 1 to 2m (3¼–6½ ft.) of water, increasing to 7 to 9m (23–30 ft.) deep. The depth marks a spectacular display of coral creations, colorful schooling fish, and spotted eagle rays; even resident turtles can be found.

Even closer for most guests staying on Grace Bay is **Bight Reef,** located in the Grace Bay area known as the Bight, just offshore from the Coral Gardens resort. A roped-off circle of buoys is there to keep the area from further degradation, so you simply snorkel your way around the rope. The coral is sun-bleached, but you'll see plenty of action even in the shallowest areas (the water depth ranges from 1–5m/3¼–16 ft.). You'll noodle about in the water amid schools of bright yellowtail snappers, glorious green parrotfish, lumbering hawksbill turtles, and the occasional barracuda.

On **North Caicos,** the snorkeling is excellent at Three Mary Cays, a marine sanctuary just east of Sandy Point and part of 11km-long (7-mile) Whitby Beach. On **Middle Caicos,** you can snorkel near Pelican Cay off Bambarra Beach.

BEACH EXCURSIONS & BOAT CHARTERS

One of the most popular watersports activities in the Provo area is a **beach excursion ★★**, offered by a number of tour operators. These excursions—often on spacious power catamarans—come in any number of variations and combinations, and in many instances you can personally tailor your own excursion or hire a private charter to take you to a secluded cay for the day.

Charter boats leave from **Heaving Down Rock Marina,** on Provo's northeast shore, or **Turtle Cove Marina,** but most operators include hotel or resort pickup and drop-off in the price of your excursion—and in many instances that means pickup directly on the beach.

A favorite beach excursion is a half-day or full day out on the Caicos Cays that includes **snorkeling, a visit to Iguana Island** (see box below), and a **shelling stopover** on one of the uninhabited cays. Other variations include **conch diving** (you can try to dive the 6m/20-ft. depths, but most people let the expert guides do the diving to retrieve fresh conch) and a subsequent lunch of fresh conch salad, prepared on the spot ceviche-style; **beach barbecues or picnics;** or **sunset cruises** with wine and cheese.

On a **glowworm cruise,** boats take you out around sunset 4 or 5 days after a full moon to see millions of mating glowworms light up the shallow local waters with a glittering green glow.

More ambitious beach excursions include **"island safaris"** and **eco-tours,** trips that may combine boating and snorkeling with caving, bird-watching, kayaking, biking, hiking, visiting historic sites, or having lunch in a native home. **Big Blue Unlimited** (www.bigblueunlimited.com; ✆ **649/946-5034**) is highly recommended for its creative eco-tours.

Day trips to uninhabited islands like **East Caicos, East Bay Islands National Park,** and **Joe Grant Cay** are becoming increasingly popular. These trips may involve snorkeling, exploring ruins, bird-watching, fishing, and any number of cool castaway activities. Amphibious Adventures (http://amphibiousadventures. org; ✆ **649/232-2588**) and **North Caicos Boats** (www.north caicosboats.com; ✆ **649/232-4141** or 649/947-7470) specialize in customized excursions to these remote Middle, North, and East Caicos islands.

A Visit to Iguana Island

Many of the beach excursions to the Caicos Cays include a short tour of **Little Water Cay** ★, a protected nature reserve (part of the Princess Alexandra National Park) and home to the **Turks and Caicos rock iguana,** a small, harmless reptile that is found nowhere else but in the TCI. Boardwalks and observation towers have been constructed at two popular landing sites to reduce the impact of tourism—this is, after all, one of the most popular attractions in the Turks and Caicos. As you walk along the wooden boardwalks that crisscross the 47-hectare (116-acre) island, you'll spot members of the island iguana population, here some 3,000 strong, emerging from their sand burrows. The biggest of these iguanas are more than .6m (2 ft.) long and solid; they're handsome fellows, if you like the rough-and-ready type, and rule the roost. The rock iguanas of Turks & Caicos are the islands' largest native land animal—even so, they're no match for a number of predators, including cats. About 50,000 rock iguanas remain here, the largest and healthiest population in the Caribbean. A park access fee of $5 per visitor goes to the Turks & Caicos National Trust to help support further conservation activities.

Most watersports operators offer **private charters,** whether for personalized island touring or just a pickup or drop-off on another island.

For contact information on recommended operators who offer excellent beach excursions and private charters, go to the "Caicos Watersports Operators: Master List," earlier in this chapter.

SAILING, PARASAILING & OTHER WATERSPORTS

KAYAKING   You can kayak the gentle ocean swells along Grace Bay (most resorts have ocean kayaks) or farther afield. **Big Blue** (www.bigblueunlimited.com; ✆ **649/946-5034**) offers kayaking eco-tours and custom kayak adventures among the interlinking cays and mangrove channels in and around the Caicos Cays, North Caicos, and Middle Caicos.

KITEBOARDING & WINDSURFING   Kiteboarding—also known as kitesurfing—has really taken off in the Turks and Caicos. Conditions for this sport are excellent: The calms waters are protected by a coral reef, the seas are uncrowded, and winds can be very cooperative. You can get kiteboarding and windsurfing lessons

2

Sailing, Parasailing & Other Watersports

EXPLORING PROVO & THE CAICOS ISLANDS

and/or equipment rentals directly on Grace Bay Beach from **Windsurfing Provo** (in front of the Ocean Club East resort; www.windsurfingprovo.tc; ☎ 649/241-1687). Windsurfing rates are $40/hour and $150/day. Also recommended is **KiteProvo** (www.kiteprovo.com; ☎ 649/242-2927), with IKO- and PASA-certified instructors Mike Haas and Terri Tapper. Both Windsurfing Provo and KiteProvo offer 3-hour Kiteboarding Fundamentals lessons for $250/per person an hour. **Big Blue** (www.bigblueunlimited.com; ☎ 649/946-5034) also offers windsurfing and kiteboarding expeditions, lessons, and rentals.

PARASAILING You won't see jet skis blazing across Grace Bay, but you may see billowy parasails skimming the clouds. It's quite a sight: colorful parasails casting shadows on the aquamarine seas. Ask your resort concierge for recommended parasail operators; at press time the go-to company was **Sky Pilot Parasail** (☎ 649/333-3000), but parasail operators tend to come and go. A 15-minute flight over Grace Bay costs $75.

SAILING Sailing excursions are offered by many charter groups, most notably **Sail Provo** (www.sailprovo.com; ☎ 649/946-4783). It sails 14m or 15m (48-ft. or 52-ft.) catamarans on half- or full-day excursions. One of the most frequented is a half-day sail and snorkel for $68 per person ($40 children 3–11) that's offered on Monday, Wednesday, and Saturday and includes a tour of Little Water Cay, or "Iguana Island." A full-day cruise from Tuesday through Friday costs $150 per person ($80 children 3–11), including a

---

Spotting JoJo the Dolphin

JoJo, a wild Atlantic bottlenose dolphin, is a local celebrity here and acts like one, showing off for visitors as he plays in the local waters. He's even a movie star, having appeared in *Nature* and *In the Wild: Dolphins,* both PBS specials, and the 2000 IMAX film *Dolphins.* He's so famous that he's been named a Turks & Caicos National Treasure and as such enjoys protected status. He likes to trail boats, and covers quite a bit of ground; he's been seen on Grace Bay and Middle Caicos alike. A whole cottage industry of all things JoJo has sprung up. You can learn more about JoJo and the JoJo Project on the website of the **Marine Wildlife Foundation** (www.marinewildlife.org), which is dedicated to the research and preservation of dolphins, whales, and all marine wildlife. If you see JoJo while dining at Hemingway's oceanfront restaurant at the Sands at Grace Bay resort, a bell is there to ring for the occasion.

lunch buffet served onboard. Sail Provo also offers sunset cruises and glowworm cruises.

A retired rumrunner, *Atabeyra,* is owned by **Sun Charters** (www.suncharters.tc; ℂ **649/231-0624**). Happy hour sunset cruises cost $39 per person. Customized private charters can be arranged for half- or full-day trips and include food, drinks, snorkeling gear, and sailing down the chain of Caicos Cays, perhaps following an ocean trail blazed by Columbus. A kid-pleasing 3-hour Pirate Cruise goes to Treasure Island and costs $49 to $59.

You can also sail aboard the catamaran **Beluga** (www.sailbeluga. com; ℂ **649/946-4396**), on which Captain Tim Ainley leads small, personally tailored beach excursions or private charters for romantic beach barbecues.

STAND-UP PADDLEBOARDING The Turks and Caicos have ideal conditions for stand-up paddleboarding, one of the fastest-growing board sports in the world. It's pretty much what the name implies: You stand in the center of a thick surfboard and propel yourself through the water with a long paddle. You can cruise the flat or gentle swells along the shoreline or peaceful mangrove channels. It's a total body workout—as well as a balancing act. Most resorts are now stocking stand-up paddleboards with their other beach toys. If not, **Windsurfing Provo** (in front of the Ocean Club East resort; www.windsurfingprovo.tc; ℂ **649/241-1687**) has stand-up paddleboards to rent ($25/hour; $75/day). **Big Blue,** always at the forefront of eco-sensitive activities, offers stand-up paddleboarding expeditions and rentals (www.bigblueunlimited. com; ℂ **649/946-5034**).

 Day Pass at Beaches

Even if you're not staying there, you can treat yourself and your family to a day's worth of all the resort activities, meals and drinks, and encounters with *Sesame Street* characters you can possibly stand with a day pass to the all-inclusive **Beaches Turks & Caicos Resort & Spa** (p. 68). The cost is $200 per adult ($130 per child) and lasts from 9am until 5pm. It's an especially fun option for the small kids in your party who are gaga for all things Elmo and Cookie Monster—and not a bad day at the beach for older kids who have total access to Beaches' wealth of sports and watersports facilities—including the Pirates Island Waterpark, with seven water slides, a lazy river, a waterfall pool, and a Surfstream simulator—and the Xbox 360 Game Garage. For details, call ℂ **649/946-8000.**

2

Sailing, Parasailing & Other Watersports

EXPLORING PROVO & THE CAICOS ISLANDS

FISHING

The fish are biting in the Turks and Caicos, where the waters are ripe for bonefishing, reef fishing, deep-sea fishing, and bottom fishing. The bonefishing in particular is world-class. A number of excellent boat-charter companies offer fishing expeditions; see "Caicos Watersports Operators: Master List," earlier in this chapter, for contact information.

If you'd prefer a more personalized fishing experience, we highly recommend hiring a local fishing guide to take you out. In Middle Caicos, **Dolphus Arthur** (© **649/946-6122**) is one of the island's top fishing guides, as is his brother **Cardinal Arthur** (© **649/946-6107;** cellphone 649/241-0730). On North Caicos, contact **Nat Gardiner** (© **649/241-4838**), who's been fishing the local waters for 40 years.

Note that fishing is not allowed in the country's national marine parkland.

Bonefishing

The elusive "ghost" of sparkling saltwater flats, the bonefish is the ultimate prey for many fishermen, and chasing the ghost the ultimate hunt. The Lorimer flats in Middle Caicos in particular contain thousands of acres of virtually untouched saltwater flats where the bonefish is king. Fishermen have reported spotting potential world-record fish in the Middle Caicos flats on every trip.

The fastest and easiest way to access these shallow, remote waters is by airboat. With one of only two airboats on the island, **Blue Horizon Resort** (http://bhresort.com; $400–$500 half-day trip; rental equipment available) can quickly deliver fishermen to places even locals have never been. It's a 20-minute ride from the resort to put the airboat in the water, and then a 10-minute ride to the fish.

"It's a pure thing, to catch a bonefish," says Adam Craton, Blue Horizon's resident fishing guide. "It's not easy. They're very elusive and spook easily. It's not really fishing; it's hunting."

Deep-Sea Fishing

For those who'd like to venture farther afield, half- and full-day deep-sea fishing expeditions are available, with all equipment included. Catches turn up wahoo, tuna, kingfish, marlin, and even shark. **Grand Slam Fishing** (www.gsfishing.com; © **649/231-4420**) offers fishing charters for big game in its 46-foot Hatteras boat. Half-day deep-sea-fishing charters run around $1,200 per group (six to eight people maximum) or $250 per person on a shared charter. Full-day trips cost around $2,200.

GOLF & TENNIS

In a country that currently has only two golf courses (on Provo and Grand Turk), the golf scene is somewhat limited. However, rumors persist that the Northwest Point area will get a golf course in the near future.

GOLF Provo Golf & Country Club ★, on Grace Bay Road (www.provogolfclub.com; ✆ **649/946-5833**), is a 6,560-yard, par-72, 18-hole course designed by Karl Litten of Boca Raton, Florida, and owned by the Turks and Caicos Water Company. It is powerfully green and—because Provo is one of the driest spots on the globe—it takes an extraordinary amount of water to keep it that way. Young palms and bougainvillea, as well as rocky outcroppings and powdery sand traps, help make the course a challenge to the serious golfer or a lovely day on the links for the beginner or novice. Four sets of tees allow golfers to tailor a game to their level of expertise. A driving range and putting greens are also available. Inside the newly renovated clubhouse is a full-service restaurant and bar called **Fairways Steakhouse** (p. 51).

Greens fees are $180 per person for 18 holes. The price includes the use of a shared golf cart, which is mandatory. Golf clubs can be rented for $30 to $60 per set. The course is open from 7am to dusk daily. The course also has two lighted hard tennis courts (see below). Inside the clubhouse is the Pro Shop, a fully stocked store with golf and tennis equipment as well as tennis and golf shoes, collared shirts, tailored shorts, and hats.

TENNIS Many of Provo's hotels and resorts have on-site tennis courts, including Beaches, Club Med, the Grace Bay Club, the Ocean Club, the Palms, and the Sands at Grace Bay. The **Provo Golf & Country Club** has two floodlit hard courts that non-members are welcome to reserve ($20 per adult [$14 16-and-under juniors] per hour; reserve 24 hr. in advance; daily 7am–7:30pm).

EXPLORING THE ISLANDS
Providenciales

Provo offers little in the way of historic or cultural attractions; for a real feel for the rich heritage of the TCI, you'll need to head to North or Middle Caicos (see below) and, of course, to Grand Turk and Salt Cay (see chapter 5).

Caicos Conch Farm ★ THEME PARK/FARM/TOUR This attraction and working conch farm is back up and running again after suffering severe damage in the hurricanes of 2008. Conch has many natural predators—man is at the top of the list—and only a tiny percentage of hatched conch eggs survive in the wild, whereas 25% of the eggs survive here in this controlled environment. The staff gives visitors a short walking tour of the breeding basins—included is a tour of the hatchery and the laboratories. The tour is modest, but the passion for the cause is palpable.

Leeward Hwy., Providenciales. (C) **649/232-5119.** $10 adult, $5 children. Mon-Fri 9am–4pm; Sat 9am–2pm.

Cheshire Hall ★ RUINS Many of the Belongers who live on these islands are descendants of slaves brought here by British Loyalists in the 18th century to build and work vast cotton plantations. Cheshire Hall was built by a Loyalist named Wade Stubbs from Cheshire County, England. He and his brother William grew sea-island cotton on thousands of acres of land until the crop was exhausted in the early 1800s. The ruins of the Great House sit atop a lush, overgrown hill, surrounded by the crumbling remains of outbuildings, once-bustling engines to the cotton trade. The Turks & Caicos National Trust runs guided tours Monday to Friday 8:30am to 4pm; call to arrange a tour.

Off Leeward Hwy., Providenciales. www.nationaltrust.tc. (C) **649/941-5710.** Tours $5 per person.

North Caicos

A number of charter-boat operators offer island tours, eco-tours, bird-watching tours, plantation tours, and private charters to North Caicos, including **Big Blue Unlimited** (www.bigblueunlimited. com; (C) **649/946-5034**). Big Blue combines boat rides with bike trips, kayaking, bird-watching, and lunches in native homes to get deep into the North Caicos experience.

Flamingo Pond ★ NATURE RESERVE Just southeast of Whitby, on the main road, is the Flamingo Pond overlook. During certain times of the years, the pond is a massive cloud of pink. These tidal flats are home to the largest protected nature sanctuary of West Indian flamingos on the islands. Bring binoculars for close-up glimpses; the overlook is some distance from the pond.

Kings Rd., Whitby, North Caicos.

Wades Green Plantation ★ RUINS North Caicos became plantation country when Americans loyal to the British Crown (Loyalists) fled the United States to come here, where they were provided property from the British Crown, in the wake of the War of Independence. According to historians at the Turks & Caicos National Museum, in 1788 the Caicos islands had a population of over 40 white families and 1,200 slaves. All slaves were freed in 1834, and today many descendants of these slaves reside in North

Caicos. The main industry on these plantations was growing sea-island cotton, an endeavor that eventually failed as a result of dry conditions, thin soil, pests, and tropical storms. Today you can still see the occasional cotton plant growing tall along the roadside in both North and Middle Caicos. Outside of Kew are the ruins of one of the most successful plantations of the Loyalist era, Wades Green, which was constructed by Florida Loyalist Wade Stubbs around 1789 and eventually grew to 1,214 hectares (3,000 acres). Today you can see the ruins of the stone house, outbuildings, and surrounding walls, pillowed in North Caicos scrub brush. Call the Turks & Caicos National Trust for tours. The ruins lie about a mile off the main road turnoff.

Kew, North Caicos. ℂ **649/946-5710.**

Middle Caicos

Big Blue Unlimited (www.bigblueunlimited.com; ℂ **649/946-5034**) combines boat rides with bike trips, kayaking, swimming, and cave exploration on Middle Caicos. Middle Caicos native and guide **Cardinal Arthur** (ℂ **649/946-6107;** cellphone 649/241-0730) offers informative caving, bird-watching, fishing, eco-, and general sightseeing tours of the island. Also offering cave tours (and good general sightseeing tours) is local guide **Ernest Forbes, Sr.** (ℂ **649/946-6140**).

Middle Caicos is also the site of **British Colonial plantation ruins.** Plantation crops of cotton and sisal drove the island economy from the late 1780s until slavery was abolished. The ruins of **Haulover Plantation,** one of the largest Loyalist plantations in the country, lie down the unpaved road to Haulover Point. You'll have to walk through tangled vegetation to get to the ruins; just follow the crumbling stone wall.

Conch Bar Caves National Park ★★ NATIONAL PARK   This massive limestone cave system is a treat to discover on sunbaked TCI, sprawling for 15 miles aboveground and studded with impressive stalactites, stalagmites, flowstone, and pools. Artifacts found in the cave date from the occupation of pre-Columbian Lucayan Indians more than 600 years ago (see the display of Lucayan artifacts in the Turks & Caicos National Museum). Today the caves are basically a home for bats (mined for exported guano back in the late 19th c.), and land crabs, which skitter around the cave entrances. *Tip:* Bring along mosquito repellent. Tours of the caves are offered by eco-tour operators like **Big Blue Unlimited** and local guides (see info above). For more information, contact the **Turks & Caicos National Trust** (http://tcinationaltrust.org; ℂ **649/946-5710**).

Bush Doctor, Poet & Artist

As you drive to the end of Lorimors Road, you will know you have arrived in the little village of Lorimers by the painted buoys and floats hanging in the trees and hand-painted signs bearing inspirational messages. When his wife died several years ago, It's said, Mr. Alton R. Higgs started dressing up the place a bit. He combs the beach for usable materials and concocts bush medicine out of native plants. Mr. Higgs is now into his 90s, but he is happy to give local tours and talk about growing up in little Lorimers, now home to just a handful of folks. You can't miss his house—it's the one with messages written hither and thither—and a sign lets you know if Mr. Riggs is in.

The Crossing Place Trail ★★ HISTORIC SITE/WALKING TRAIL This historic coastal route, much of it tracing a bluff above the spectacular azure waters of Mudjin Harbor, was first established in the late 1700s by cotton plantation settlers. As part of the Turks & Caicos National Trust Middle Caicos Ecotourism Project, the trail has been cleared and reopened from the Conch Bar to the Indian Cave field road. "Crossing Place" refers to the sandbar-strewn spot where in years past people crossed at low tide to reach North Caicos. During the days of the Loyalist plantations, the owners rode in carriages along the King's Road while the slaves walked the breeze-filled coastal trail. You can hike or bike this trail; go to **www.tcimall.tc/middlecaicos/crossingplace.htm** for more information on hiking and biking routes. The trail is generally flat, with some low hills, and there are plenty of places to take a swim along the way. For more information, contact the **Turks & Caicos National Trust** (http://tcinationaltrust.org; *C* **649/946-5710**).

SPAS & GYMS
Spas

The resorts of Providenciales and the Caicos Cays have some of the finest spas in the Caribbean region—and at many, you don't even have to be a resort guest to take advantage of some truly splendid treatments. (You'll need to reserve any spa treatment in advance, of course.)

Here is a sampling of some of the top resort spas in the TCI that welcome nonguests. Be sure to ask whether a service charge has been added to your bill (some places automatically tack on service charges of up to 18%).

Anani Spa   This is the Grace Bay Club's full-service spa, and it already boasts some of the top massage therapists on the island. The spa specializes in Euro-Asian spa techniques, and treatments range from "aroma stone therapy" to deep-tissue massage to ocean wraps. You can get a treatment in one of the six indoor treatment rooms or outdoors in one of two beach spa tents. Massage treatments run from $130 to $360; the spa is open daily from 9am to 7pm (6pm in summer). Call **649/946-5050,** ext. 1045, for appointments.

COMO Shambhala   Many people think this is the finest spa in the Caribbean, and it's hard to argue otherwise. The 613-sq.-m (6,600-sq.-ft.) space at the Parrot Cay resort is wrapped in a sea of glass that looks out over the island wetlands. Inside, free-standing wooden pavilions are treatment salons where Eastern-influenced healing and rejuvenating therapies are applied by Balinese healers. Call *©* **649/946-7788** for appointments, or visit http://parrotcay.com.

Exhale Spa   Bringing big-city spa treatments to Provo, Exhale Spa (www.exhalespa.com), at the Gansevoort Turks + Caicos, offers fusion massage, couples' massage, deep tissue massage, and body scrubs, as well as facials, manicures, pedicures, and brow and body waxing. Call *©* **649/941-7555** for reservations. Massages run from $115 to $290.

The Regent Spa at the Regent Palms   You'll feel better just stepping into this place, which is elegant and soothing all at once. It's simply a beautiful space, classically designed around reflecting pools. Some of the treatment rooms are set in alfresco coral-stone cabanas shaded by palm trees. The menu of services is extensive and includes facials, massages, body scrubs and other therapies, and day retreat packages (the Regent Palms resort, Grace Bay, Providenciales; www.regentturksandcaicos.com;

Day-Tripping to Parrot Cay

You can enjoy the superlative spa experience at COMO Shambhala (above) by arranging a **day trip** to the island. The cost for the boat transfer is $100 per person, and you can eat lunch in the Lotus restaurant or enjoy the lovely beach or the pool while you're there—the extra costs of food, tips, and spa treatments are on you, of course. Call to reserve a treatment and arrange a boat transfer, which departs from the resort's own dock at Leeward. Massages run from $190 to $300.

② **649/946-8666,** ext. 30208 or 30211). Massages start at $135; it's open daily from 8:30am to 8pm.

The Thalasso Spa at Point Grace   The ambience is absolutely dreamy: outdoors in an open-air structure with beach views and sea breezes. This full-service European-style thalassotherapy spa uses the properties of seawater as well as applications of sea mud and select seaweed in its body and facial treatments. The menu includes Swedish massage, shiatsu, body scrubs, and wraps (Point Grace Resort, Providenciales; www.pointgrace.com; ② **649/946-5096,** ext. 4126). It's open daily 9am to 6pm. Massages cost $75 to $180.

Gyms

Many resorts have on-site gyms or fitness centers. For those that don't, the **Athletic Club** (formerly Pulse Gym; the Saltmills, Grace Bay Rd.; http://athleticclubnet.com; ② **649/941-8686**) is open 7 days a week and has Cybex strength and cardio equipment; free weights; and exercise, Pilates, and yoga classes.

SHOPPING

Providenciales and the Caicos islands are still a work in progress when it comes to shopping, although an increasing number of small shopping "villages" or plazas have cropped up along Grace Bay Road, including the **Ocean Club Plaza, Regent Village,** and **Le Vele plaza.** Other, older shopping plazas include the **Saltmills** (Grace Bay Rd.), which has seven shops, including a wine-and-liquor store, and several restaurants; **Ports of Call** (Grace Bay Rd.), with eight shops and several restaurants; and the **Graceway Shopping Center** (Leeward Hwy.), with the big IGA Graceway Supermarket, a bookstore, and several shops.

You may not be shopping until you drop during your TCI vacation, but you can discover some real gems if you do some digging—particularly when it comes to regional artwork, much of it reasonably priced and including the famously colorful paintings by artists from neighboring Haiti, as well as local crafts, such as Middle Caicos fanner-grass baskets and silvertop-palm bags and handmade model sailboats. A new crop of artists is designing jewelry out of sea glass and other beach-combed treasures. And with **Salt Cay Salt Works** (http://saltcaysaltworks.com), Salt Cay's salt is back (the Salt Cay salt industry was once the world's premier salt provider) and has been beautifully packaged, whether as Fleur de Sel, bath salts, or soap.

Most shops are open from 9 or 10am to 5 or 6pm (generally later in the high season), but hours are ultimately subject to the owners'

SHOPPING THE hotel BOUTIQUES

Shopping doesn't have to stop at your hotel door. A number of hotels and resorts in Provo have very good in-house boutique shops, many selling gorgeous goods you won't find elsewhere in Provo—and even in most standard-issue hotel gift shops. Here are a few recommended shops and a sampling of the stuff you might discover there. For a map of these resorts, see chapter 4.

o **Amanyara:** This hotel resort on Provo's Northwest Point offers such high-end goodies as Asian-inspired tunic tops and Amanresorts' wonderful spa products.

o **Beaches:** Beaches has two stores: **Treasure Island,** which sells high-end beachwear, Beaches-branded T-shirts, hats, and beach paraphernalia, gifts, snacks, soft drinks, and limited toiletries; and **Pirate Cove,** which sells *Sesame Street*–branded clothes and toys and other kids' items.

o **The Gansevoort:** Not surprisingly for this cosmopolitan brand, this boutique sells sexy (and pricey) styles in swimwear and silky kurtas, among other high-end products.

o **The Meridian Club:** This small shop sells Meridian Club T-shirts, tops, and hats, locally crafted basketry, and other gift items.

o **The Palms:** Palm Place, which faces the terrace of restaurant Parallel23, is a real shopping mecca, featuring not one

whims. Be sure to call in advance so you aren't disappointed to find that a store has shut down for the day.

Artwork

Art Provo ★ This art gallery has a large selection of paintings by local artists, TCI pottery, baskets, jewelry, and glass. Look for local painters like Dwight Outten (cousin of Phillip Outten, another well-known native painter), a Middle Caicos native whose colorful, linear oil paintings of the region are particularly fine; Pamela Leach, who paints colorful island-scapes; and Susan Moore, who paints island scenes on Middle Caicos driftwood. Look for locally made jewelry fashioned from Grand Turk beach glass. Regent Village, Grace Bay Rd., Providenciales. http://artprovo.tc. ✆ **649/941-4545.**

Maison Creole In addition to Haitian arts and crafts, including hand-painted place mats and boxes, this airport shop has greatly expanded its inventory of locally made crafts, including Middle Caicos baskets, Salt Cay salt products, and jewelry from local but five boutique shops. **Wish** boutique has upscale clothing, including those sweet little soft cotton tops and skirts from designer James Perse. Next door, the **Palm Shop** carries casual logo wear and gift items. **Splash** has beachwear. **Spice** has gourmet snacks and beverages, such as Harry and David chocolate-covered cherries and Miss Vickie's Potato Chips. **Harmony Gallery** sells lots of the home furnishings and pricey little tchotchkes (handblown-glass conch shells, sea-urchin candlesticks, shell-encrusted mirrors) you see around the hotel. (Oh, and you can also buy skincare products and treatments along with big-ticket yoga- and sleepwear in the **Spa at the Palms.**)

o **Parrot Cay:** The shop sells lovely but pricey jewel-encrusted Asian-style tunics and kurtas, along with other high-end clothing, books, jewelry, bags, and a few essential toiletries. The COMO Shambhala spa's wildly popular Invigorate line of soaps, shampoos, and the like is also on sale here.

o **Somerset on Grace Bay:** This nice little boutique is packed with beachwear, sundries, salt and salt products from Salt Cay, and other local souvenirs.

artisans. International Departures Lounge, Providenciales International Airport, Providenciales. ✆ **649/946-4285.**

Books

Unicorn Bookstore   This, the island's only full-service bookstore, has books (bestsellers, fiction, nonfiction, kids' books, and more), newspapers, magazines, and gifts. Leeward Hwy., in front of the IGA Graceway, Providenciales. ✆ **649/941-5458.**

Clothing

Caicos Wear   This small clothing store offers a good selection of comfortable casual wear, sundresses, colorful peasant skirts, bathing suits, and bags. La Petite Place, Grace Bay Rd., Grace Bay. ✆ **649/941-3346.**

Dive Provo   This dive operator's shop offers dive trips and snorkeling equipment, plus some stylish casual tops and shorts that work well in a tropical clime. Ports of Call shopping plaza, Grace Bay Rd., Providenciales. www.diveprovo.com. ✆ **649/946-5040.**

Handicrafts

Ground was broken in 2012 for the construction of a Providenciales campus of the **Turks & Caicos National Museum** (http://tcmuseum.org). If the gift shop in the museum in Grand Turk is any indication, this will offer some of the best souvenir shopping in the Turks and Caicos.

Middle Caicos Co-op ★ Handsome hand-carved model Caicos sailing sloops can be custom-ordered from the Middle Caicos Co-op—sail plan, size, and color schemes all to your specifications. These sloops are carved from the native gum-elemi tree, a Caribbean softwood. The co-op also sells fanner-grass baskets, silvertop-palm straw hats, bags, and more, plus Middle Caicos grits. The co-op is closed in much of the off season; be sure to call ahead to make sure it's open even in high season. Conch Bar, Middle Caicos. www.tcimall.tc/middlecaicos/co-op.htm or e-mail middlecaicos@tciway.tc. ©/fax **649/946-6132.**

Turks & Caicos National Trust Shop ★ Here you can find the real deal: crafts and products made in the Turks and Caicos, including native pottery, fanner-grass baskets, silvertop-palm bags, model Caicos sloops, and more. Get your rock iguana T-shirts here! IGA Graceway Plaza, Leeward Hwy., Providenciales. http://tcinationaltrust.org. © **649/941-3536** or 649/941-5710 (main office).

Jewelry

Jai's This duty-free shop sells a number of big international brands, including Cartier, Bulgari, David Yurman, Movado, and TAG Heuer. It also has locations in the international-departures lounge in the Provo airport and in the Grand Turk Cruise Center. Regent Village, Grace Bay Rd., Providenciales. www.jais.tc. © **649/941-4324.**

ENTERTAINMENT & NIGHTLIFE

The nightlife on Provo can't begin to compete with the late-night sizzle of, say, Aruba or St. Maarten. The TCI is a fairly conservative place overall, where the party vibe is laid-back and easygoing, but a variety of quality nighttime diversions can be found.

BEACH SHACKS The **beach shacks along Blue Hills Beach** are great places to drink Turk's Head beer or a little rum, eat conch, and listen to music. On Friday nights, Da Conch Shack has a Dancing in the Sand party.

BEACHSIDE BARS Providenciales has some terrific beachside lounges or bars from which you can watch the sun set. Two of the best are the Grace Bay Club's **Lounge,** with white-cushion seating and glowing fire pit, and its sister lounge the **Infinity Bar** (© 649/946-5050), with its gleaming black marble bar—the longest in the Caribbean—stretching toward the horizon. The **Beach Lounge** at the Gansevoort is an attractive gathering spot. Also visit the bar/lounge/deck at **Amanyara** (© 649/941-8133), the **Plunge** pool bar (the Regent Palms resort; © 649/946-8666), and any of the **Blue Hills beach shacks** (see the "Head for the [Blue] Hills" sidebar, in chapter 3).

CASINOS   The casino action can be found at the laid-back **Casablanca Casino,** which offers roulette, blackjack, craps, and baccarat and is open from 1pm to 5am (Grace Bay Rd., Providenciales; www.thecasablancacasino.com; © 649/941-3737).

GOLF COURSE BAR   The **Fairways Bar** at the Provo Golf & Country Club (© 649/946-5833) is a pleasant place to have a drink and munch on hearty bar food.

IRISH PUB   Danny Buoy's (Grace Bay Rd., Providenciales; www.dannybuoys.com; © 649/946-5921) features a full bar stocked with imported beers on tap, darts, and pool tables; it also doubles as a sports bar showing big-time sporting events on satellite TV. Danny Buoy's has solid food, with dishes from across the pond (bangers and mash, Irish stew) as well as island fare (jerk chicken).

LIVE MUSIC   Most of the island's bars and restaurants host live-music nights. Catch live music on the terrace at **O'Soleil** (© 649/946-5900) at the Somerset resort Saturdays; reggae during sunset cookouts on the deck at the **Alexandra** (© 649/946-5807); and live music at **Hemingway's** (© 649/941-8408) 3 nights a week.

MARINA BARS   Turtle Cove Marina in the northwest section of Provo has a number of jolly dockside bars with happy hours (5–7pm) and good pub grub, both bar snacks and full-service menus. Join in the fun at **Banana Boat** (© 649/941-5706), the **Tiki Hut Cabana Bar** (© 649/941-5341), and the **Sharkbite Bar & Grill** (© 649/941-5090).

SPORTS BARS   Club Sodax is a lively sports bar with a good mix of locals and tourists (Leeward Hwy., Providenciales; © 649/941-4540). **Jimmy's Dive Bar & Grill** (in the Port of Call shopping plaza, Grace Bay Rd., Providenciales; http://jimmys divebar.com; © 649/946-5282) is another popular spot where you can watch sports on big-screen TVs.

WINE BAR   It's a treat to sip wine or a cocktail on a wooden deck overlooking the glittering lights of Turtle Cove and beyond at

Magnolia Restaurant & Wine Bar (📞 649/941-5108), with an impressive lineup of wines.

Movie Theaters

L'Raye Cinema (www.lrayecinema.com; 📞 649/941-3541), at Windsor Place on Leeward Highway, is the islands' only movie theater, opened in Provo in late 2007. It was named for the former first lady of the TCI, Hollywood actress LisaRaye McCoy Misick.

WHERE TO EAT IN PROVIDEN-CIALES & THE CAICOS ISLANDS

You will eat very well in Provo—the quality and freshness of the food is remarkable for an island that has to import just about everything in its larder. But you will pay a price to do so. It's not easy to eat on the cheap here: Fast-food restaurants and chain eateries are virtually nonexistent. It helps that most hotel rooms come with fully equipped self-catering facilities—a way to offset the costs of paying for double-digit-entree meals. Many resorts offer complimentary breakfasts as well, either full American style or continental.

You can sample cuisines from around the world here, from Italian to Thai to Japanese. You'll find a number of chefs melding classic European techniques with Caribbean flavors. If it's island food you're craving, head to Provo's Blue Hills (see "Head for the [Blue] Hills," later in this chapter) or the less-traveled islands like Middle and North Caicos, where casual spots serve such Caribbean favorites as peas 'n' rice (or peas 'n' hominy); cod fish cakes; fried grouper; stewed fish; curry chicken; johnnycakes (a sweet pan bread); all things conch (conch fritters, conch chowder, and conch ceviche); and all things lobster (in season). The food is fresh, tasty, and well-prepared, and you won't pay an arm and a leg for it. Look for fresh-caught local seafood (lobster, grouper, or cracked conch at places like Daniel's Café by the

Buying Spirits in the TCI

Beer, wine, liquor, and liqueurs are sold at grocery stores, convenience stores, and liquor stores (see "Shopping for Self-Catering: Provo," below, for store locations and contact information), but no alcohol is sold in these venues on Sunday. Beer, wine, and liquor are available 7 days a week in restaurants and bars. While you're on the islands, be sure to try the local beer, **Turk's Head,** produced in a microbrewery in Providenciales. It comes in a light lager and amber. *Note:* The legal drinking age is 18 on the islands.

Sea in Middle) or traditional island meals prepared by celebrated home cooks (such as the Pelican Beach Hotel on North Caicos, where owner Susie Gardiner is happy to cook up the day's catch).

What will you eat that actually *comes from* the Turks and Caicos? Like many other arid islands in the region, the TCI grows little of its own food. The exception is fertile North Caicos, where farms like Green Acres, Caicos Farm, and the Government Organic Farm are growing sweet peppers, hot peppers, tomatoes, callaloo, herbs, okra, squash, and papaya for sale on island. But most of what you eat in Provo restaurants is imported. A Provo hydroponic farm has in the past provided restaurants with fresh lettuce, cucumbers, tomatoes, and herbs. The true local bounty comes from the sea, in the form of fresh conch, Caribbean lobster (in season, Aug–Mar), and a range of great-tasting fish from the local waters, such as red snapper, grouper, and mahimahi.

Keep in mind that the government adds an 11% tax on all restaurant bills. Some resort restaurants also tack on a 10% (and higher) service tax. Always check your bill before tipping to make sure a gratuity has not already been included in the total.

In general, Providenciales and the Caicos islands are not late-night dining destinations. Most restaurants stop serving between 9 and 10pm and close down altogether by 11pm. The dress code in the TCI is casual for the most part, although some of the top-end restaurants recommend "resort elegant" attire.

PROVIDENCIALES

Most of the dining choices in Provo are found in the Grace Bay area. Turtle Cove and the Blue Hills also have restaurant options; see listings below and the "Head for the (Blue) Hills" box later in this chapter.

Have a full kitchen at your fingertips? Stock it with the following self-catering options. Located smack-dab in the center of Provo's Grace Bay is **Graceway Gourmet** (www.gracewaygourmet.com; ℰ **649/941-5000**), at the corner of Grace Bay Road and Dolphin Avenue, which sells all the basics—meats, vegetables, fruits, snacks, drinks—as well as a thoughtful selection of gourmet goods. The larger Graceway store, the **Graceway IGA** (www.gracewayiga.com; ℰ **649/941-5000**) is on Leeward Highway. You can buy fresh fish and lobster straight from **South Dock** (lobster season runs from Aug–April); arrive at 3:30 or 4pm when the boats come in—but don't go after dark and always be aware of your surroundings. All grocery and convenience stores sell liquor, beer, and wine, but if you're looking for a wider selection, head to the **Wine Cellar** (ℰ **649/946-4536**) on Leeward Highway. Keep in mind that alcohol is sold every day but Sunday. **The Kissing Fish** (www.kissingfish.tc; ℰ **649/941-8917**), **Caicos Catering** (www.caicoscatering.com; ℰ **649/231-6890**), and **Gourmet Catering** (www.gourmetcatering.tc; ℰ **649/941-4141**) offer full-service party catering (weddings, beach barbecues, birthdays) and will prepare and serve catered gourmet dinners in your villa or condo.

If you have no car and the restaurant is not within walking distance, have your hotel call a taxi for you. For more information on getting around, see chapter 6.

Blue Hills

At press time it was unclear whether **Horse-Eye Jack's,** the popular Blue Hills beach bar and restaurant, would reopen. Check the local listings when you arrive.

Moderate

Da Conch Shack ★ CONCH/CARIBBEAN   This popular spot is set in and around a whitewashed beach shack on a sandy bluff above the Blue Hills beach. It's separated from the open-air **Rum-Bar** by sand and white picnic tables. Down below, in the aquamarine waters, small pens hold live conch, refreshed daily by fishermen. Conch this fresh and well-prepared is a revelation, and here it's served a variety of ways: as superb conch fritters, conch curry, or conch chowder. Equally good are the curry chicken, the lobster (in season), the shrimp, and the local grouper. Some people

Restaurants in Providenciales & the Caicos Islands

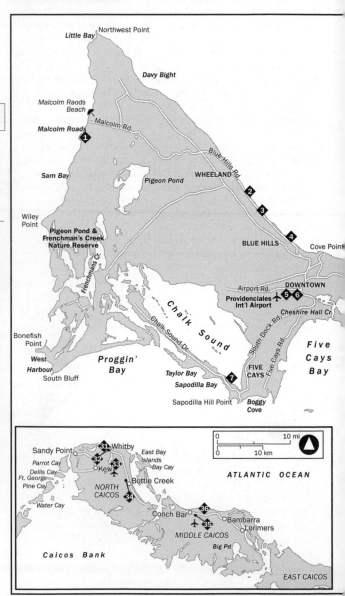

PROVIDENCIALES

Anacaona **27**
Atlantic Bar & Grill **11**
Baci Ristorante **8**
Banana Boat Restaurant **8**
Bay Bistro **17**
Bella Luna **22**
Caicos Café **24**
Coco Bistro **25**
Coyaba Restaurant **26**
Da Conch Shack **4**
Fairways Bar & Grill **29**
Froggies on da Beach **3**
Grace's Cottage **19**
Hemingway's on the Beach **18**
Hole in the Wall **5**
Jimmy's Dive Bar **23**
Las Brisas **7**
Lemon Café **21**
Magnolia Restaurant &
  Wine Bar **9**
Mango Reef **13**
Matsuri Sushi Bar **12**

Mother's Pizza **6**
O'Soleil **16**
Parallel23 **15**
Pelican Bay Restaurant & Bar **28**
Restaurant at Amanyara **1**
The Restaurant at the
  Gansevoort **10**
Rickie's Flamingo Cafe **30**
Smokey's on the Bay **14**
Three Queens Bar &
  Restaurant **2**
Tiki Hut **8**
Vix Bar & Grill **20**

NORTH CAICOS

Miss B's Island Hut **34**
My Dee's Restaurant & Bar **33**
Pelican Beach Hotel **31**
Silver Palm **32**

MIDDLE CAICOS

Daniel's Café by the Sea **36**
Dillon's **35**

come straight here from the airport, kick off their shoes, and order up a platter of conch and an icy Turk's Head lager.

Blue Hills. www.conchshack.tc. ✆ **649/946-8877.** No reservations. Conch, fish, chicken, and shrimp dishes $12–$14; lobster $28. MC, V. Daily 11am–9pm.

Chalk Sound
EXPENSIVE

Las Brisas ★★ CARIBBEAN/MEDITERRANEAN You'll need a car or a taxi to reach this gorgeous spot, about a 15-minute drive from the Provo airport (and a 25- to 30-min. drive from the Grace Bay resorts) on Chalk Sound. You can sit inside or on the terrace for breathtaking views of the sound's cerulean waters. You can even take a sunset cruise on a pontoon boat (call for reservations and rates). Las Brisas has an extensive island-style tapas menu; you can make a meal out of such delicacies as shrimp in garlic, fish ceviche, lobster wontons, and chickpeas with chorizo. The restaurant has a number of reasonably priced options and a handful that will especially appeal to kids, such as baskets of fish fingers and chicken fingers. Mains range from rich pastas to local seafood cooked any way you like it to hefty cuts of meat.

Neptune Villas, Chalk Sound, Providenciales. www.neptunevillastci.com. ✆ **649/946-5306.** Reservations recommended. Main courses $16–$36; T-bone steak $42. AE, MC, V. Wed–Mon 11am–10pm; closed Tues.

Downtown
MODERATE/INEXPENSIVE

Hole in the Wall ★ JAMAICAN/CARIBBEAN This popular Jamaican restaurant on Old Airport Road has some of Provo's best island food, from excellent jerk chicken and pork to fried fish, curry goat, and barbecued ribs. Sides include peas 'n' rice and fried plantains. Breakfast is the real island deal, with seasoned codfish, cornmeal porridge, peas 'n' grits, and johnnycakes. Hole in the Wall even offers free pickup/drop-off service to and from Grace Bay accommodations.

Downtown at Williams Plaza, Old Airport Rd. ✆ **649/941-4136.** No reservations. Main courses $12–$16. No credit cards. Daily 7am–11:30pm.

Grace Bay

For Mediterranean-style cuisine in a sultry Moroccan-style setting (belly dancing included), the **Lemon Café,** in the Village at Grace Bay (✆ **649/941-4059;** dinner Mon–Sat), is an excellent choice. Sample such Mediterranean specialties as lamb moussaka, grilled kabobs, chicken *tagine,* and tabbouleh salad.

What It Costs: Bottle of Turk's Head Beer	
Graceway Gourmet (Provo)	$2.00
Regent Palms Spice Shop (Provo)	$3.50
Liquors Plus (North Caicos)	$2.50
Dillon's Café (Middle Caicos)	$4.00
Grand Turk Liquors (Grand Turk)	$2.50
Jack's Shack Beach Bar (Grand Turk)	$5.00
Island Thyme restaurant (Salt Cay)	$6.00

VERY EXPENSIVE

Anacaona ★★★ CARIBBEAN/EUROPEAN Set beneath thatched-roof *palapas* and the starry evening sky, this is one of Provo's top restaurants, with a fantastic location directly facing Grace Bay Beach. Steps away are the resort's two buzzing bars, the **Lounge** and the **Infiniti Bar,** where you can sip a cool drink before dinner and watch the sun melt into the Atlantic. Tabletop candles and the flickering lights from free-standing torches deepen the romantic mood. The menu changes regularly, but you might start with a tempura tuna roll; fire-roasted sweet potato soup; or crab, chorizo, and corn risotto. Main courses focus heavily on seafood, particularly fish—try the Caribbean spiced mahimahi or the jerk- and rum-marinated Chilean sea bass. No children 4 or under.

In the Grace Bay Club, 1 Grace Bay Circle Rd. www.gracebayresorts.com. © **649/946-5050.** Reservations recommended. Main courses $32–$49. AE, MC, V. Daily 6:30–9pm.

Coco Bistro ★★★ MEDITERRANEAN/CARIBBEAN This perennial favorite is set in a former plant nursery that has since grown into the largest palm grove on the island. It's a magical spot: You dine outside under the palms, candles twinkling. The food is as memorable as the ambience. Sample tasty starters such as conch, garlic, and potato soup scented with saffron; grilled shrimp satay on sugarcane skewers; and avocado and lobster spring rolls. For a main, try the roast rack of Colorado lamb with an herb crust or a seafood pasta loaded with shrimp, scallops, and asparagus in a white wine tomato cream sauce.

Grace Bay Rd. www.cocobistro.tc. © **649/946-5369.** Reservations recommended. Main courses $28–$39. DISC, MC, V. Tues–Sun 5:30–10:30pm.

Coyaba Restaurant ★★ CONTINENTAL/CARIBBEAN Chef Paul Newman is still flexing his inventive culinary chops in this perennially popular restaurant on the gazebo-style patio fronting the Caribbean Paradise Inn. It ain't cheap, but it's mighty tasty:

Newman's culinary flair is on full display in preparations of fresh island seafood, in particular. His West Indian dishes show a strong European influence. Start with coconut tempura shrimp in Barcelo honey rum sauce or the conch and seafood chowder. As far as main courses go, the fish dishes are exuberantly flavored; the Coyaba-style lobster thermidor is formidable.

Next to the Caribbean Paradise Inn, Grace Bay. http://coyabarestaurant.com. ℂ **649/946-5186.** Reservations required. Main courses $32–$39. AE, MC, V. Wed–Mon 6–10pm.

Grace's Cottage ★★ CARIBBEAN/CONTINENTAL   This buttery-yellow cottage with Victorian-style gingerbread trim and latticework is pure enchantment. The restaurant seats 62 people, but most nights, it's filled with hand-holding couples soaking up the palpable romantic ambience. Inside you can enjoy an aperitif at the mahogany bar before dinner. Dine on the cottage terrace or on one of the patios nestled in tropical vegetation and twinkling lights. Executive chef Vincent Poitevin prepares food that is both flavorful and satisfying. You might start with the Thai shellfish bisque or the crab claw ravioli; mains include a seared filet of snapper with Caribbean conch and the crispy lamb Wellington.

In the Point Grace Hotel, Grace Bay. www.pointgrace.com. ℂ **649/946-5096.** Reservations required. Main courses $23–$40. AE, MC, V. Daily 6:30–10:30pm.

O'Soleil ★★ INTERNATIONAL/ISLAND   This showcase space, enveloped in white and accented with marble floors and crystal chandeliers, is a bit of a departure from the tropical island–style interiors of other local spots. At its best it's coolly elegant; at its worst it veers into Carmela Soprano territory. I prefer to dine on

Celebrating the Conch

The Caribbean Queen conch may be endangered elsewhere, but here in the Turks and Caicos, it's plentiful and a tasty and versatile staple. It's prepared and served raw, fried, curried, jerked, and even candied. Get a memorable taste of Queen conch and Blue Hills hospitality at the annual **Turks & Caicos Conch Festival,** held the last Saturday in November. Local restaurants vie to win top honors for best versions of various conch concoctions, including conch chowder, conch curry, and conch salad, to name a few. In 2010 the Best in Festival honor was awarded to Bay Bistro (p. 50) for the second year in a row. In its ninth year, the conch festival has become a real party, with music, food, conch-blowing contests, and a heavenly Blue Hills beach location. For more information, go to **www.conchfestival.com.**

the alfresco terraces; the patio out front faces the green croquet lawn, and the Zen Garden on the restaurant's backside is enveloped in bamboo and has soothing waterfall walls. A new chef is preparing the menu created by the now-departed Lauren Callighen, and early reports indicate that things are going swimmingly. Start with the tequila-cured salmon or the pistachio-crusted scallops. Entrees include a curried grouper in a lime curry sauce; a Caribbean shrimp tagliatelle; and terrific New York steak, here in a wild-mushroom demi-glace. The service is superb.

In the Somerset on Grace Bay resort, Grace Bay. www.thesomerset.com. *©* **649/946-5900.** Reservations recommended. Main courses $26–$40. AE, DC, MC, V. Daily 7–10:30am and 6–10:30pm.

Parallel23 ★★★ TROPICAL FUSION/INTERNATIONAL Parallel23 enjoys an elegant perch on the first floor of the Mansion, the Regent Palms resort's stately homage to Caribbean Great Houses of old, and cultivates an appealing garden-party ambience. Try to snag a table on the terrace, entwined in flower vines and lit by gas lamps specially ordered from New Orleans. Overlooking the glittering Palm Place courtyard, it's a bewitching spot. The menu balances top-end foods (impeccably sourced aged steaks and Wisconsin veal) with creative nightly specials. It's a thoughtful menu, with lots of nifty touches (the butter is whipped with Parmesan and truffle oil). Starters include yellowfin tuna sashimi and pan-seared foie gras. From the grill menu, choose your grilled meat, sides, and toppings. The attached **Green Flamingo Bar** (open noon–midnight) has the kind of overstuffed sofas and dark-grain wood that would be right at home in a gentleman's club in some colonial outpost.

In the Regent Palms resort, Grace Bay. *©* **649/946-8666.** Reservations required. Main courses $18–$38. AE, MC, V. Daily 7–10:30am and 6–10:30pm.

The Restaurant at the Gansevoort ★★ FRENCH MEDITERRANEAN With nods to South Beach and downtown Manhattan, this urbane spot serves a Continental menu in a good-looking, monochromatic indoor/outdoor space dotted with towering palm trees. The ambience is crisp and relaxed all at once, with an up-tempo soundtrack that heats up as the day progresses. But in the evening, when the sky is a canopy of stars and shadows dance in the breeze, you are very much aware that you are in Provo—and Provo at its most seductive. The kitchen is still a work in progress, but meat dishes such as the porterhouse pork chop are impeccably prepared. The fish is also recommended; sample local grouper or pan-roasted wahoo with leeks and crabmeat sautéed in a brandy white wine butter sauce.

In the Gansevoort Turks + Caicos, Lower Bight Rd. www.gansevoortturksand caicos.com. ℂ **649/946-5746.** Reservations recommended. Main courses $29–$46. AE, MC, V. Sun–Thurs 7am–10pm; Fri and Sat 7am–11pm.

EXPENSIVE

Caicos Cafe ★★ MEDITERRANEAN Even without sea views, this has long been an island favorite for its romantic ambience. Caicos Café is set on the terrace deck of a sunny Caribbean cottage trimmed with gingerbread, twinkling lights, and palm fronds. It's located on Grace Bay Road, within convenient walking distance of several Grace Bay resorts. New chef Max Olivari has taken the reins and completely revamped the menu. Start with your choice of carpaccio (usually fish of the day or salt-baked beef tenderloin). Pastas include linguine with clams and zucchini and *orecchiette* with sausage, eggplant, broccoli, and cherry tomatoes. Mains include grilled fish, lobster, ribs, and sirloin.

Caicos Café Plaza, Grace Bay Rd. ℂ **649/946-5278.** Reservations recommended. Main courses $18–$36. MC, V. Tues–Sat noon–2pm; Mon–Sat 6–10pm. Closed Sept–Oct and 2 weeks in June.

MODERATE

Atlantic Bar & Grill ★ 🍴 CARIBBEAN This modest and unpretentious outdoor bar and grill has something like nine tables and a limited menu—but it's a little gem. The restaurant has little room for food storage, so everything's delivered fresh daily. The chefs (one of whom cooked for Dubai royalty) prepare tasty and fresh island specialties, not to mention a creamy shrimp linguine and a nice fat rib-eye steak; daily specials depend on what rolled into the pantry that morning. An outdoor grill is employed to cook up pizzas, cheesecakes, pies, even cookies. The bar is small but very convivial.

In the West Bay Club resort, Lower Bight, Grace Bay. www.thewestbayclub. com. ℂ **649/946-8550.** Main courses $24–$35. AE, MC, V. Daily 7:30–10:30am, 11:30am–3:30pm, and 6–9pm.

Bay Bistro ★★ CARIBBEAN/EUROPEAN The location here is pretty fantastic, directly overlooking Grace Bay. It's a sweet, casual spot, set in a whitewashed wooden open-air porch above the beach, and management has taken advantage of the setting by setting up additional beachside tables, lit by flaming torches. The food is good and hearty, featuring an assortment of standard Caribbean specialties (conch fingers, fish wrap, snapper, tuna, and mahimahi), steak, chicken, and rack of lamb. Grilled lobster in season is all you want it to be. Tasty starters include terrific conch wontons and crepes of Princess conch and mushroom. The Bay Bistro serves food practically all day long, from breakfast to dinner; have a drink in the restaurant bar, **Junior's Bar,** and sample

Junior's award-winning concoctions. Service, at one time a sore spot in an otherwise winning experience, is much improved and considerably more congenial.

In the Sibonné Beach Hotel, Grace Bay. www.sibonne.com. ☎ **649/946-5396.** Reservations recommended. Main courses $27–$35; surf and turf $65. AE, MC, V. Daily 7am–10pm.

Bella Luna ★ ITALIAN   Situated up in "the glass house" on a slight rise along Grace Bay Road, Bella Luna provides yet another of Provo's many romantic dining experiences. The restaurant is a Provo old-timer, serving food since 1996. Chef Cosimo Tipodi gives his Italian menu a few subtle Caribbean tweaks. You can start with beef carpaccio or conch *frittelle* (grilled conch patties with a jerk mayo sauce). Veal and chicken are served a number of classic Italian ways. Pastas are recommended, particularly seafood pastas like the linguine *tuttomare,* with fresh lobster (in season only) and shrimp with your choice of sauce: marinara, cream, or rosé. Linguine *marechiaro* is basically linguine in clam sauce with a spicy kick to it. Weekday lunch is served in high season only.

Grace Bay Rd., Grace Bay. ☎ **649/946-5214.** Reservations recommended. Main courses $22–$30. AE, MC, V. Mon–Sat 6–10pm.

Fairways Steakhouse ★★ 🍴 STEAK/CONTINENTAL   With all the ocean-side dining available in Provo, why on earth would you want to dine on a golf course? Well, to see what new chef Lauren Callighen (formerly of O'Soleil) is up to, for starters. Fairways has always had a lively atmosphere, what with the comings and goings of golfers and tennis buffs. In fact, you can eat here all day if you really want—the restaurant is open for breakfast, lunch, and dinner. The bright, airy, high-ceilinged space has French doors that open onto an outdoor terrace with seating overlooking the 18th green. The menu is extensive; choose from hand-cut selections of dry-aged beef, preparations of local fish, and solid desserts.

Provo Golf & Country Club, Grace Bay Rd. ☎ **649/946-5833.** Reservations requested. Main courses $16–$28. AE, MC, V. Daily 7am–9pm.

Hemingway's on the Beach ★ CARIBBEAN/INTERNATIONAL   This casual open-air place is reliably good, and the ocean-side location is a big plus. Yes, for a certain discriminating diner used to drinking a certain kind of house wine, Hemingway's comes up short. But the Turk's Head beer is frothy and refreshing, and the coconut shrimp light and tasty. If it's in season, order Hemingway's grilled lobster, which arrives at the table with a buttery char. Hemingway's is also a fine lunch choice, serving a terrific mango shrimp salad over Provo lettuce with mango chutney, a very respectable hamburger, and satisfying chicken and chips: marinated and fried Caribbean jerk chicken breast with the restaurant's signature seasoned fries. At night, torches and candlelight heighten the romance. A bell mounted on a pole is there to be rung by anyone who spots JoJo the resident dolphin cruising Grace Bay (p. 27).

At the Sands at Grace Bay. www.thesandstc.com. ℂ **649/941-8408.** Reservations required. Main courses $19–$36. AE, MC, V. Daily 8am–10pm.

Mango Reef ★★ ☺ CARIBBEAN/INTERNATIONAL This cheerful, laid-back spot has hit the beach, leaving its longtime location overlooking the pool at the Royal West Indies Resort for the sun-splashed sands of Grace Bay. In its new location at the Alexandra Resort, Mango Reef is still serving delicious food at relatively reasonable prices in an unstuffy fashion, attracting both tourists and TCI movers and shakers. It's a big menu, with plenty of seafood, including conch (fritters, salad, and cracked) and a piquant snapper curry. Caribbean pork comes with fresh pineapple salsa. At lunch you can choose between panini, pizza, burgers, sandwiches, and Caribbean specialties. It's a kid-friendly spot, too. And ah, those sea breezes!

At the Alexandra Resort, Princess Dr., Grace Bay. www.mangoreef.com. ℂ **649/946-8200.** Reservations recommended. Main courses $21–$34. AE, MC, V. Daily 8am–10pm.

Matsuri Sushi Bar ★ SUSHI/JAPANESE Sushi lovers swear by the sushi served at this island outpost, next to the Graceway IGA. You can get set dinners of sushi, sashimi, rolls, or combos. A number of rolls are available, from standard California to spicy octopus. This may be one of the few places in the sushi world where you can get a conch maki. The owners also operate a restaurant in the Saltmills on Grace Bay Road, **Yoshi's Japanese Restaurant** (ℂ 649/941-3374), with a similar menu and similar hours.

101 Graceway House (next to the Graceway IGA), Leeward Hwy. ℂ **649/941-3274.** Main courses $14–$39; sushi rolls $6–$16. DISC, MC, V. Mon–Sat noon–3pm and 6–10pm.

Pelican Bay Restaurant & Bar ★★ CARIBBEAN/CONTINENTAL Taking over the old Mango Reef location is this solid newcomer overseen by Chef Peter Redstone, whose culinary path has taken him from London to the Regent Palms' Parallel23, the Grace Bay Club's Anacaona, and now the Royal West Indies Resort. Pelican Bay offers a "local menu" of island favorites like curried fish, North Caicos fried chicken, and conch chowder, and Mediterranean-style "chef specialties" such as lamb Provençal and pasta pesto primavera. Lobster tails come grilled in a Guinness-infused jerk sauce.

Royal West Indies Resort, Grace Bay. www.pelicanbaytci.com. ℂ **649/941-2365.** Main courses $16–$38. AE, MC, V. Daily 7:30am–10pm.

HEAD FOR THE (blue) hills

The welcoming beach-shack bar/restaurants along the Reef Harbor shoreline of northwest Provo represent what one local describes as an authentic "taste of old-time Provo." For a therapeutic immersion in the TCI art of studied languor, you can't beat a meal at one of the shacks in Provo's oldest settlement along the rural Blue Hills road, dotted with pastel-painted churches and schools. In fact, many visitors come here straight from the airport, kicking off their cold-weather armor and city-slicker shoes to dig toes into warm sand, stare out at sun-dappled azure waters, and dine on conch fresh from the sea. Even better, the food you get at these shacks is TCI home cooking. The oldest of the Blue Hills bars, **Three Queens Bar & Restaurant** is a favorite hangout, especially on Saturdays and Sundays, where you can sample fresh fish and join the locals in a spirited game of dominoes (℡ 649/941-5984; Mon–Fri 9am–11pm, Sat 8am–9pm, and Sun noon–9pm). At **Da Conch Shack** (p. 43), dine on conch fritters and sip rum from the RumBar. One of the newest beach bars, **Froggies on da Beach** (℡ 649/231-0959), has a Wednesday-night cookout. **Smokey's on the Bay** (℡ 649/241-4343), a long-time Blue Hills bar/restaurant favorite, is now located across the street from the Alexandra Resort on Grace Bay. Check to see if **Horse-Eye Jack's** and **Sailing Paradise** are open on your visit.

Rickie's Flamingo Cafe ★ CARIBBEAN   At press time, the food herd was converging on the beach between Club Med and Ocean Club East resort (at the sign for Opus) at Rickie's Flamingo Cafe, a beach shack painted in lime and lemon hues and serving up flavorful native cuisine. It's a refreshing alternative to the upscale eateries along Grace Bay. Sample curried grouper, cracked conch, and grilled lobster, and peruse the souvenirs sold by island vendors, who share the **Cultural Market Place** building with the cafe from 9am to 5pm. Or just come for a sunset cocktail on a fine stretch of beach.

Cultural Market (Grace Bay Beach, btw. Club Med and Ocean Club East).
℡ **649/242-7545** or 247-5496. Main courses $12–$28; burgers, sandwiches, and salads $10–$14. MC, V. Daily 10am–late.

Vix Bar & Grill ★ MEDITERRANEAN   It may not have the best location on Grace Bay—it's tucked in the Regent Village shopping plaza on Grace Bay Road—but Vix has made up for that with a handsome, atmospheric interior and an intriguing menu. The creative choices include seafood curry, slow-roasted pork belly, corn and crab risotto, and a carefully curated wine list. You can dine outside on the attractive landscaped patio.

Regent Village shopping plaza, Grace Bay Rd. © **649/941-4144.** Main courses $18–$32; lobster (in season) $36. AE, MC, V. Daily breakfast, lunch, and dinner.

INEXPENSIVE

Jimmy's Dive Bar AMERICAN   Jimmy, a New Yorker who got fed up with life in the Big Apple, runs this lively little sports bar and grill. Its kitchen stays open later than most to feed the folks who arrive in Provo on the last flights of the day. It was Jimmy's intent to create a Provo version of a diner and, in keeping with the diner ethos, breakfast, lunch, and dinner are served. This is probably the only place on the island where you can get both a Philly cheese sub *and* cracked conch. Happy hour is 4 to 7pm daily.

Ports of Call shopping plaza, Grace Bay Rd. © **649/946-5282.** Sandwiches $11–$17; main courses $12–$45. MC, V. Sun–Wed 9am–11pm; Thurs–Sat 9am–midnight.

Mother's Pizza PIZZA   Craving pizza after a week of conch? Voted "Best Pizza in Provo," Mother's serves up 18-inch pies in classic fashion or gourmet style (try the Mac & Cheese Pizza or the Loaded Potato Pizza). Mother's charges a $5 delivery fee to resorts and businesses in Grace Bay and Turtle Cove.

Times Square, Airport Rd., Downtown Providenciales. http://motherspizzatc. com. © **649/941-4142.** 18-in. pizzas $20–$25. Mon–Sat 11am–11pm; Sun 4–9pm.

Northwest Point
VERY EXPENSIVE

Restaurant at Amanyara ★★ ASIAN/MEDITERRANEAN The restaurant in the Amanyara resort accepts nonguests, but you must reserve a day in advance. The menu features Asian- and Mediterranean-infused cuisine (with an emphasis on local seafood); you can eat indoors or on a terrace overlooking the water at Northwest Point. Arrive early to have a drink on the bar terrace and watch the sun set.

Amanyara Resort, Providenciales. www.amanyara.com. © **866/941-8133.** 40 private pavilions. Main courses average $45. AE, MC, V. Daily 6–10:30pm.

Turtle Cove
EXPENSIVE

Baci Ristorante ★ ITALIAN   This spot enjoys one of the prettiest waterside settings in Provo, on the docks of the Turtle Cove Marina. Lacy iron doors lead out to terraced outdoor seating overlooking the water. The tasty cuisine, the romantic patio, the stone floors and wrought-iron entrance, and the whirling *Casablanca*-style overhead fans make dining here an agreeable experience. Veal is served any number of ways: in lemon butter sauce, in a red-wine peppercorn sauce, in a Marsala-and-mushroom sauce, or baked and topped with a tomato demi-glace and mozzarella. The hearty pasta dishes include the usual suspects: fettuccine Alfredo, for example, and penne a la vodka (here with chicken). Baci also has kid-friendly brick-oven pizza, with plenty of toppings to choose from.

Turtle Cove Marina, Harbour Towne. ℂ **649/941-3044.** Reservations recommended. Lunch $10–$18; main courses $19–$27; call for lobster prices. AE, MC, V. Mon–Fri noon–2pm; Mon–Sat 6–10pm; closed Sun.

Magnolia Restaurant & Wine Bar ★★ MEDITERRANEAN/ ASIAN/INTERNATIONAL You won't find a setting like this anywhere else on Provo: high on a hill overlooking Turtle Cove Marina, with the sparkling lights of the island spread out before you. You could almost be dining in a cliff-side trattoria overlooking the Mediterranean. Magnolia has established itself as one of the top places to dine in Provo, with chef Matt Gaynor continuing the tradition of excellence. Start with a bracing version of TCI–style seafood chowder, tempura shrimp, or a stack of grilled vegetables and mozzarella. Try the sesame seed and cracked pepper crusted rare seared tuna or the bacon-wrapped, pesto-stuffed pork tenderloin.

At the Miramar Resort, Turtle Cove Marina. ℂ **649/941-5108.** Reservations recommended. Main courses $24–$34. AE, MC, V. Tues–Sun 6–10pm. Wine bar opens at 5pm.

MODERATE

Banana Boat Restaurant CARIBBEAN/SEAFOOD The Banana Boat is not the best restaurant on the island, but it's certainly one of the most convivial—there's not a yachtie on Provo who hasn't moored here to enjoy a tasty island meal and a potent tropical drink. For a main course, you might try T-bone steak, cracked conch, or freshly caught local fish. At lunch, favorites include lobster salad or a half-pound burger. No one in the kitchen fusses too much with these dishes, and here that's a good thing. A choice seat is on the timber-and-plank veranda that juts out over piers on Turtle Cove. On Tuesdays, prices for all entrees are cut in half, and Saturday is karaoke night.

Turtle Cove Marina. ℂ **649/941-5706.** Lunch $6.50–$15; main courses $12–$26. AE, MC, V. Daily 11am–11pm.

Tiki Hut ★ CARIBBEAN My friends from the fine state of Washington swear by the flavorful, unfussy food at Tiki Hut and in particular recommend the famous Chicken & Ribs Night every Wednesday. It's a grand bargain indeed, at $13 a head, and the baby back ribs are saucy and delicious. This friendly, casual spot is located dockside at Turtle Cove Marina, frequented by the usual harborfront gumbo of boaters, bar hounds, families, and lovers of tasty, unfussy food.

Turtle Cove Marina. © **649/941-5341.** Reservations only for parties of 5 or more. Main courses $17–$33. AE, MC, V. Mon–Fri 11am–11pm; Sat–Sun 11am–10pm.

NORTH & MIDDLE CAICOS

The dining options in North and Middle Caicos are slim, but all offer excellent opportunities to sample traditional TCI cuisine in casual, laid-back settings. And because most of these establishments are small and rely on what the fishermen are catching that day, you should call ahead and reserve a table. Keep in mind that most of these restaurants keep reduced hours in the off season. All of the following serve beer, wine, and some liquor.

North Caicos

Miss B's Island Hut CARIBBEAN Miss B is Bernestine (Berni) Gardiner, and this sunny, high-windowed space just off Airport Road is open for breakfast, lunch, and dinner. Everything is made to order, and you can get breakfast all day long, along with free Wi-Fi. For a real island breakfast, come on weekends, when the special is pork or chicken souse served with homemade johnnycakes. Miss B's conch chowder is a thick, buttery brown stew flecked with carrots and onions. For dinner, order the delicious garlic shrimp or choose between blackened, pan-fried, or grilled fish. The catch of the day is whatever fisherman and local guide Nat Gardiner (Miss B's father) brings in from the sea. Ask about fishing and boating excursions led by Mr. Gardiner.

Airport Rd., North Caicos. © **649/946-7727.** Reservations recommended for dinner. Main courses $18–$25 dinner; $8–$12 lunch. AE, DISC, MC, V. Mon–Sat 7am–closing (8–10pm in peak season); Sun 8:30am–4pm.

My Dee's Restaurant & Bar CARIBBEAN This sprawling local hot spot serves up fresh-caught local fish for lunch or dinner, and on Friday nights the action spills outside, where barbecue grills smoke and sizzle with spare ribs and chicken. For lunch, choose the fish fingers: generous chunks of flaky fried grouper with sides of rice and salad.

My Dee's Mini Mall, Airport Rd., North Caicos. © **649/245-1239.** Dinner by reservation Mon–Thurs. Main courses $17–$18; grilled lobster with vegetable or mashed potato $25; steak and lobster with sides $30. DISC, MC, V. Mon–Tues 7:30am–4pm; Wed–Sat 7:30am–11pm.

Both North and Middle Caicos have few resources for buying food and drink. But Middle Caicos is particularly limited, with no supermarkets or gas stations, just a handful of mom-and-pop sundries shops. You'll need to stock up on food, drink, and essential supplies in Provo or North Caicos before you arrive in Middle or have your resort or villa do it for you. In North Caicos, you can buy groceries and sundries at **KJ Foods** (𝄞 **649/946-7705**), in Whitby (just past Big Josh MacIntosh's bar); or at **My Dee's Variety** (𝄞 **649/243-2344**), on Middle Street in Bottle Creek. A good supply of beer, wine, soda, and liquor can be found at **Liquors Plus** (𝄞 **649/946-7761**), in My Dee's Mini Mall in Bottle Creek.

If you're staying in North and craving fresh fish (or want to catch your own), call **Nat Gardiner** (𝄞 **649/241-4838**), who's been fishing the local waters for 40 years. In Middle, a number of local fishermen can supply you with fresh fish and lobster; call **Dolphus Arthur** (𝄞 **649/946-6122**), one of the island's top fishing guides. Visitors staying on North and Middle Caicos can buy fresh vegetables direct from the farm at the newly reinvigorated **Government Organic Farm** in Kew (the farm road is potholed and rocky) and **Green Acre Farm** in Bottle Creek. It's also worth checking whether delicious Middle Caicos grits are on sale in the **Middle Caicos Co-op** (𝄞 **649/231-4884**).

Pelican Beach Hotel CARIBBEAN   The restaurant at the Pelican Beach Hotel serves delicious homemade meals prepared by the owner, Susie Gardiner, who has a deft touch with seafood. Note that you must call ahead to reserve a table.

In the Pelican Beach Hotel, North Caicos. www.pelicanbeach.tc. 𝄞 **649/946-7112.** Reservations required for dinner. Main courses $10–$20. DISC, MC, V. Tues–Sun 11:30am–2:30pm.

Silver Palm CARIBBEAN   This colorful restaurant offers a menu that includes conch dishes (chowder, fritters, cracked conch), grilled or pan-fried fish, lobster (in season), and homemade breads and desserts.

North Caicos. http://oceanbeach.tc. 𝄞 **649/946-7113.** Reservations and preorders required for dinner. Main courses $19–$32; surf and turf $38. MC, V. Open for breakfast, lunch, and dinner. Open Nov–June only.

Middle Caicos

Daniel's Café by the Sea ★ CARIBBEAN   You'll need to call ahead to reserve a table (and choose your entree) at this small but congenial spot right next to the Crossing Point Trail. Daniel O. Forbes and his son Devon serve up delicious local seafood (cracked conch, pan-fried fish, breaded wahoo) along with Daniel's famous peas 'n' rice, salad or coleslaw, and homemade bread. Lobster in season (Aug–Apr) comes perfectly grilled in a garlic butter sauce. You can eat inside or out on the deck (you'll need bug spray if there's no breeze). Be sure to stop in next door at the **Middle Caicos Co-op,** which sells such locally made crafts as model sailing sloops and fanner-grass baskets.

Conch Bar Village, Middle Caicos. ⓒ **649/946-6132** or 649/246-4809. Reservations required for all meals. Full dinner $35–$45 per person; full lunch $20. DISC, MC, V. Tues–Sun 11am–4pm; closed Mon. Closed Sept.

Dillon's CARIBBEAN This local joint is just across the street from the Middle Caicos airport. It has an active bar, even offering that sweet milk stout from Jamaica, Dragon Stout. But the kitchen turns out solid island grub, including ribs, fried chicken, and fried or grilled snapper; both come with peas ' rice and salad.

Middle Caicos Airport, Middle Caicos. ⓒ **649/242-2983.** Reservations required for dinner. Lunch platters $10–$12; dinner $15 and up. Cash preferred. Mon–Sat 8am–4pm; closed Sun.

WHERE TO STAY IN PROVIDEN- CIALES & THE CAICOS ISLANDS

4

Things are pretty swell along the sweeping sands of Provo's celebrated 19km (12-mile) beach, Grace Bay. For the most part, Grace Bay is the home of low-rise, high-end resorts with boutique-style amenities. The prevalence of upscale resorts in Provo means that consumers looking for a budget island getaway should reserve well in advance for the handful of moderately priced options.

It's also useful to be on the lookout for package deals on hotel websites, online travel-booking sites such as Orbitz, Expedia, and Travelocity, or massive travel search engines like Kayak and Mobissimo. Check this guide's hotel reviews before you book, and see what other travelers have to say about TCI lodgings on Frommers.com message boards.

In contrast to what's available on Provo and Parrot Cay and Pine Cay (two privately owned Caicos Cays islands with hotel resorts), moderately priced lodgings are currently the main option in the rest of the Caicos islands.

Keep in mind that the government imposes a mandatory 11% occupancy tax, and many resorts charge an additional service charge of 10% or more. Also note that even though you may be staying only 1 night, many resorts require a 3-night deposit to reserve a room. Most resorts have minimum-stay requirements during

the Christmas/New Year's holidays. Hotels throughout the Turks
and Caicos accept most major credit cards, except where noted.
Just about every hotel in the TCI runs special online offers and
seasonal packages; be sure to check resort websites for the latest
deals.

Finally, as you can see when comparing winter and summer rack
rates listed below, visiting Provo in the off season is considerably
more economical than in the winter. The most expensive time to
come is during the Christmas/New Year's holidays; check each
resort's website for holiday rates. Be sure to look for money-saving
online package deals at any time of year.

For information on villa or apartment stays in Provo and the
Caicos islands, see "Tips on Accommodations" in chapter 6.

PROVIDENCIALES

When you touch down at Providenciales International Airport,
you're just an easy 10- to 15-minute taxi ride away from the island's
lodgings listed below.

Grace Bay
VERY EXPENSIVE

Grace Bay Club ★★★ ☺   This luxury boutique resort sets the
bar for exemplary service in the TCI. Opened in 1993, it's one of
the island's oldest hotels, but near-manic refreshment by one of the
Caribbean's finest management teams underscores its commitment
to excellence. You'll be pampered plenty for your money—at times
a little obsequiously—but a whopping repeat business proves

Finding Sundries on Grace Bay

For visitors who find they've forgotten an essential toiletry, crave a snack or a soft drink (and want to avoid paying through the nose in a resort restaurant or bar), or need sunscreen or bug repellent, the Grace Bay area can be a tough place to locate such little conveniences—unlike in North America, where 7-Elevens and other convenience stores and grocery chains are almost always just around the corner. Vending machines are virtually nonexistent. But now Grace Bay has a full-service grocery store. The **Graceway Gourmet** (*Ⓒ 649/333-5000**), across the street from the Seven Stars Resort in central Grace Bay (at Dolphin Ave.), is impressively stocked and more conveniently located than its (larger) sister grocery store, the Graceway IGA, on Leeward Highway (reachable by car or taxi). In addition to basic supplies like sunscreen and snacks, the Graceway Gourmet has fresh produce, meats and seafood, a salad bar, a deli, a coffee bar, and even Wi-Fi; it's open 7 days a week from 7am to 9pm. A few other well-placed convenience stores within walking distance of most resorts in and around Grace Bay supply the essentials and more, including snacks and candy bars (all the familiar brands); beer, wine, and liquor; magazines; and even local handicrafts—but the prices are more inflated than what you pay at Graceway Gourmet or the Graceway IGA. Hours can vary, but the following are generally open daily from 9am to 6pm:

o **The Sand Dollar** at the Sands at Grace Bay resort

o **Sand Castle Convenience Store** (in the Ocean Plaza, at Ocean Club East)

o **Neptune's Nectar** (behind the Ports of Call shopping village)

they're doing things right. It doesn't hurt that the resort sits on the largest oceanfront acreage on Grace Bay (4.5 hectares/11 acres).

The hotel has accomplished the neat trick of creating three hotels in one (all with fabulous Grace Bay views): a romantic **21-suite hotel** with its own pool and bar and restaurant (Anacaona); four low-density villas containing **38 upscale, family-friendly condos,** positioned directly on the beach with their own pool and restaurant (Grill Rouge); and the newest addition, the **Estate at Grace Bay Club,** with 22 custom-designed ultra-luxe oceanfront residences fronting a lap pool and a poolside bar/restaurant. The Estate's 650-sq.-m (7,000-sq.-ft.) penthouse is utterly stunning, with four oceanfront bedrooms, a media room, and terraces with sublime views.

Hotels in Providenciales & the Caicos Islands

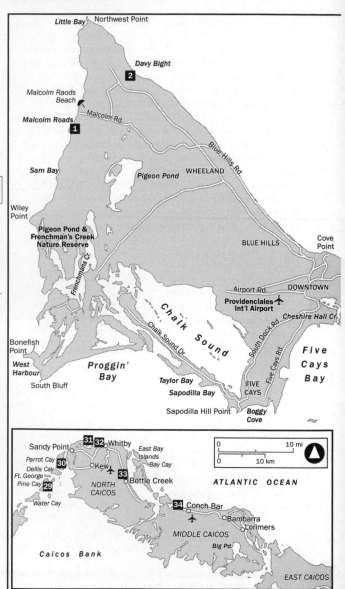

PROVIDENCIALES

The Alexandra **10**

Amanyara **1**

Beaches Turks & Caicos Resort & Spa **8**

Caribbean Paradise Inn **24**

Club Med Turkoise **27**

Comfort Suites **23**

Coral Gardens/Reef Residences on Grace Bay **7**

The Gansevoort Turks + Caicos **4**

Grace Bay Club **25**

Grace Bay Suites **16**

Le Vele **18**

Northwest Point Resort **2**

Ocean Club East **28**

Ocean Club West **22**

Point Grace **15**

Regent Grand **20**

The Regent Palms **11**

Royal West Indies Resort **26**

The Sands at Grace Bay **14**

Seven Stars Resort **21**

Sibonné Beach Hotel **13**

The Somerset on Grace Bay **12**

Trade Winds Condotel **17**

Turks & Caicos Club **6**

Turtle Cove Inn **3**

The Veranda **9**

Villa Renaissance **19**

The West Bay Club **5**

CAICOS CAYS

The Meridian Club **29**

Parrot Cay Resort **30**

NORTH CAICOS

Bottle Creek Lodge **33**

Hollywood Beach Suites **31**

Pelican Beach Hotel **32**

MIDDLE CAICOS

Blue Horizon Resort **34**

The Grace Bay Club personifies easy elegance, with a sun-burnished Mediterranean feel. Each of the villa accommodations has travertine-tile floors, custom-made imported furnishings, deep private patios, and ocean views. Each suite (except junior suites) and penthouse has its own state-of-the-art kitchen (granite countertops, stainless-steel appliances), washing machine, and dryer. Four spacious penthouses have outdoor Jacuzzis, among other luxuries. Spa specialists offer Euro-Asian treatments at the 465-sq.-m (5,000-sq.-ft.) **Spa Anani** (open daily 9am–7pm [6pm in summer]).

The hotel's main restaurant, **Anacaona** (p. 47), is one of Provo's top restaurants—but no kids 4 or under, please. Families can dine in the adjacent **Grill Rouge,** which offers casual alfresco dining with grilled seafood, panini, salads, and a kids' menu. The beach-front **Lounge,** with its Hamptons-style white-cushion seating and glowing fire pit, is one of the best spots on the island to have a cocktail and watch the sun set on Grace Bay; it now serves a tapas menu. But for sheer heat, check out the **Infinity Bar,** which boasts the longest bar in the Caribbean, a ribbon of black stone dotted with sexy blue lights.

The children's program, **Kid's Town** (for kids 5–12), offers a full menu of half- or full-day excursions, including snorkeling, sailing, eco-activities, and kayaking; a dinnertime "campout" on the beach may include hot dogs and s'mores by a campfire.

1 Grace Bay Circle Rd. (P.O. Box 128), Providenciales, Turks and Caicos, B.W.I. www.gracebayclub.com. ⓒ **800/946-5757** in the U.S., or 649/946-5050. Fax 649/946-5758. 59 units. Hotel: Winter $1,150 junior suite, $1,250–$1,750 1-bedroom suite, $2,100–$2,600 2-bedroom suite; off season $650–$850 junior suite, $750–$1,300 1-bedroom suite, $1,250–$1,950 2-bedroom suite. Villas: Winter $950 junior suite, $1,750 1-bedroom suite, $2,100–$2,600 2-bedroom suite, $3,330 3-bedroom suite, $6,050–$8,500 penthouse; off season $550–$700 junior suite, $1,050–$1,300 1-bedroom suite, $1,250–$1,950 2-bedroom suite, $1,950–$2,450 3-bedroom suite, $3,600–$6,550 penthouse. Estate: Winter $1,300–$10,000; off season $800–$7,500. Ask about Christmas holiday rates. Extra person $150–$180 per night. Rates include full breakfast. AE, DC, DISC, MC, V. Closed Sept. **Amenities:** 2 restaurants; 3 bars; bikes; fitness center; Jacuzzi; 2 outdoor pools; room service; spa; 2 lit tennis courts; watersports equipment (extensive). *In room:* A/C, ceiling fan, TV w/DVD/CD player, kitchen (excluding junior suites), washer/dryer (excluding junior suites), Wi-Fi (free).

Point Grace ★★★ This lovely boutique hotel opened in 2000 on a lyrical crescent of Grace Bay beachfront. In a little over 10 years, Point Grace has perfected an almost effortless graciousness and racked up one award after another. The motif is turn-of-the-20th-century British Colonial, and resort services and amenities are first-rate, ranging from twice-daily maid service to midday sorbets on the beach. Don't expect the joint to be jumping: Even at its liveliest (generally during cocktail hour around the pool bar), this is a haven of quiet serenity. (Some say *too* quiet.) It costs a pretty penny to stay here, but if you're looking for a place to soothe your frayed nerves against a sonic soundtrack of palm leaves rustling in the breeze, this could be the spot.

The rooms are mighty fine, with spacious one-, two-, three-, and four-bedroom suites and penthouses furnished with Indonesian teak and brightened by crisp white Frette linens. Many are decorated with 200-year-old wall hangings from India. Hand-painted tile and mahogany doors grace the rooms, and each suite has a beautifully appointed kitchen and a washer/dryer.

Tucked away in a candlelit garden is **Grace's Cottage** (p. 48), one of the island's most romantic spots to dine. The **Thalasso Spa at Point Grace** (daily 9am–6pm) is a full-service on-site spa that offers spa treatments using sea mud and seaweed, among other delicacies, in whitewashed cottages open to the sea breezes—easily some of the best massages on the island.

Grace Bay (P.O. Box 700), Providenciales, Turks and Caicos, B.W.I. www.point grace.com. (C) **888/209-5582** in the U.S., or 649/941-7743. Fax 649/946-5097. 28 units. Winter $623–$870 cottage suites, $1,194–$1,318 oceanfront suites, $1,513–$1,671 Atlantic suites, $2,048 Cotton Cay suite, $3,115–$6,484 Big Cameron Cay suite; off season $450–$495 cottage suites, $845 oceanfront suites, $1,045–$1,250 Atlantic suites, $1,481–$1,638 Cotton Cay suite, $2,074–$2,294 Big Cameron Cay suite. Ask about Christmas holiday rates. Extra person $100 per night. Rates include continental buffet breakfast; complimentary house cocktails and hors d'oeuvres at the pool bar 5–6pm; and airport transfers. AE, DISC, MC, V. **Amenities:** 2 restaurants; 2 bars; babysitting; bikes; concierge; Internet (free); outdoor pool; room service; oceanfront spa; watersports equipment. *In room:* A/C, TV, CD/DVD players, Internet (free), kitchen, minibar, washer/dryer.

The Regent Palms ★★★ Opened in early 2005, the Palms is one of Grace Bay's classiest lodgings, with some of the most handsomely appointed rooms on the island. But don't let its cool good looks intimidate you. Yes, the neo-Palladian centerpiece of the resort is referred to as "the Mansion"—but beneath that elegant facade is a congenial Turks & Caicos ambience and a level of service that few resorts on the island can match. It also has one of the Caribbean's top spas in the gorgeous 2,323-sq.-m (25,005-sq.-ft.) **Regent Spa;** many of its 17 treatment rooms are in white-tented cabanas in a classical arrangement around an outdoor reflecting pool.

The suites are generously sized with state-of-the-art kitchens and big, marble-swathed bathrooms. You can soak in a big tub with Jacuzzi jets or bathe in the open shower (a concept that may work better on paper; showers sometime soak the floor). The resort has two main gathering spots: the infinity pool and **Plunge,** the lively pool bar and lunch restaurant. Plunge has a sunken dining terrace and a swim-up bar—as you lie around the serpentine pool, you can check your e-mail and drink a toast to another tough day. The Mansion was fashioned after the theatrical Caribbean estates designed by Oliver Messel, the late British stage designer who also created Princess Margaret's "cottage" in Mustique. It has a different feel entirely—more like a Tuscan villa overlooking a moonlit summer garden. The Mansion houses a clubby wood-paneled bar and the resort's main restaurant, **Parallel23,** which serves tropical-fusion cuisine from an open kitchen. Ask for seating on the restaurant's lovely half-moon terrace, which fronts **Palm Place,** a palm-lined courtyard with shops on both sides. Get on the hotel's e-mail list for posted specials and packages.

Grace Bay Rd. (P.O. Box 681), Providenciales, Turks and Caicos, B.W.I. www. regenthotels.com or www.regentturksandcaicos.com. *©* **866/877-7256** in the U.S. and Canada, or 649/946-8666. Christmas holiday reservations: *©* **305/532-7900** or info@thepalmstc.com only. Fax 649/946-5502. 72 units. Winter $850–$900 double, $1,250–$1,500 1-bedroom suite, $2,100–$2,350 2-bedroom suite, $2,950–$3,200 3-bedroom suite; off season $625–$675 double, $950–$1,150 1-bedroom suite, $1,550–$1,775 2-bedroom suite, $2,400 3-bedroom suite. Ask about penthouse rates and Christmas holiday rates. Children 11 and under stay free in parent's room. Rates include continental buffet breakfast. AE, MC, V. **Amenities:** 2 restaurants; 2 bars; babysitting/nanny service; Conch Kritters Club; croquet pitch; fitness center (personal trainers available on request); Jacuzzi; infinity pool; room service; sauna; spa; Plexipave tennis courts; watersports equipment (extensive); yoga, Pilates, and meditation studio. *In room:* A/C, ceiling fan, TV (flatscreen LCD TVs in penthouses), full kitchens w/Viking appliances (in suites and penthouses), minibar, MP3 player and docking station, Wi-Fi (free).

The Somerset on Grace Bay ★★★ ☺ Is it just me, or is "minimalist chic" a beach-resort cliché these days? Maybe that's why the Somerset stands out, its baroque Italianate heft a striking contrast to all that sans-serif sleekness. This 6-year-old resort looks like an old-timer in the best sense, with neo-Tuscan architecture, sweeping stone staircases, and spraying fountains. Suites have thick wood doors and are furnished in a rich palette. If all this sounds prohibitively snooty, trust me: This is one of the friendliest, most relaxing spots on the island—it hums along with maximum efficiency and minimum drama. When the sun goes down, the pool is magically lit and palms rustle in the night breeze. It's the essence of tropical serenity.

The spacious rooms and suites are available in three accommodations categories: Estate, Stirling House, and Garden Cottage. The four blocks of ocean-view Estate suites comprise four full-floor suites per block (except the penthouse, which has two floors);

each suite has a Viking grill and hot tub on its balcony. The Stirling House comprises 24 units, including both standard doubles (garden views) and suites (ocean views), and the 13 Garden Cottage units are duplexes with basement garages and garden views. Every suite has Viking equipment and appliances in the fully equipped kitchens, DVD/CD surround-sound music system (even on the balconies), travertine marble floors, and personal wine coolers. The resident restaurant, **O'Soleil** (p. 48), has terrific food and service, but the elegant white-on-white interior can feel a little frosty in this tropical setting; we prefer to dine alfresco on one of the restaurant's two handsome terraces. The lap pool stretches to the sea, with reverse currents (and underwater audio). An infinity pool near the edge of the dunes is catnip to kids—and the poolside grill a natural meeting spot for families.

Grace Bay, Providenciales, Turks and Caicos, B.W.I. www.thesomerset.com. ☎ **877/887-5722** in the U.S., or 649/946-5900. 54 units. Winter $900–$1,200 1-bedroom villa/suite, $1,200–$1,600 2-bedroom villa/suite, $1,300–$2,700 3-bedroom villa/estate, $4,000 5-bedroom estate; off season $550–$700 1-bedroom villa/suite, $800–$950 2-bedroom villa/suite, $950–$1,700 3-bedroom villa/estate, $2,500 5-bedroom estate. Rates include continental breakfast. Children 11 and under (maximum of 2) stay free in parent's room. Extra person $100 per night Dec 18–Apr 23; all other dates $50 per night. AE, DISC, MC, V. **Amenities:** 2 restaurants; pool bar; babysitting/nanny service; concierge; kids' club; croquet pitch; infinity pool; room service; watersports equipment. *In room:* Zoned A/C, TV, semiprivate elevators, private outdoor Jacuzzi (Estate suites), full kitchen w/Viking appliances (in suites), MP3 docking station, Wi-Fi (free).

The Veranda ★★ ☺ This sprawling all-inclusive opened in 2010 and already feels like a classic. It's divided into two main zones: the family-friendly West Village and the adult-oriented East Village. The center of the resort is occupied by the Veranda House, an uninspired multilevel structure encircling a courtyard. Opt instead for a stay in one of the two- or three-story pastel-hued cottages. Trimmed in gingerbread, these clapboard cottages make the Veranda look more like a neighborhood in Key West than a posh resort. Wooden porches and picket fences entwined with bougainvillea complete the picture. But step inside your room, and everything's shiny and modern, with flatscreen TVs and sleek kitchens with stainless-steel appliances. Adding English-cottage charm are wainscoted ceilings and plump bedding. (Many bathrooms have showers, not tubs.) Note that some first-floor garden-view units can be dark; if that's an issue, ask for a garden room on an upper floor. Each of the eight stand-alone beachfront houses is wrapped in flower-bedecked white picket fencing, with 370 sq. m (4,000 sq. ft.) of handsomely appointed living space and its own "front yard" with a plunge pool. The Veranda covers quite a bit of territory, but intimate zones set around landscaped lawns make it feel small-townish. The main restaurant, the **Marin,** is the beating heart of the Veranda, with fire pits aglow at night, a bar illuminated in wavy blue lights, and a second-story **Sky Lounge** where you can star-gaze while you sip. The all-inclusive designation means not only taxes and service charge are covered, but food and beverages, including hearty buffets for breakfast, lunch, and dinner. The Veranda puts prices on its menu in the name of transparency, but it's led more than one guest to believe that a la carte menu items cost extra; they don't.

Grace Bay, Providenciales, Turks and Caicos, B.W.I. www.verandatci.com. ℂ **877/945-5757** in the U.S., or 649/339-5050. Fax 649/946-5758. 169 units. Winter season $760–$1,000 studio, $1,040–$1,625 1-bedroom suite, $1,340–$1,580 2-bedroom suite, $1,620–$1,880 3-bedroom suite, $4,500 and up cottage; off season $560–$760 studio, $780–$1,000 1-bedroom suite, $1,036–$1,240 2-bedroom suite, $1,276–$1,480 3-bedroom suite, $2,400 and up cottage. Rates are all-inclusive. AE, DISC, MC, V. **Amenities:** 2 restaurants; 2 bars; afternoon tea; coffee/pastry shop; babysitting; bikes; kids' program, playroom, and sandbox; concierge/personal concierge desk; fitness center; 3 pools; spa; tennis courts (lighted); watersports equipment (extensive). *In room:* A/C, TV, full kitchen (except studios), PlayStations, Sony Dream Machines, washer/dryers (except studios), Wi-Fi (free).

EXPENSIVE

Beaches Turks & Caicos Resort & Spa ★ ☺ This Grace Bay mega-resort remains a perennial favorite among families. And with a whopping 620 units, it's remarkable that it all chugs along as smoothly as it does. The grounds are handsomely maintained, kids look deliriously happy, and weddings are held on-site on an almost daily basis. It's a winning formula, and rooms are nearly impossible to come by in high season without reservations made long in advance.

This resort is part of the Sandals chain of all-inclusive hotels, though unlike most Sandals, this property welcomes kids—and welcomes them with open arms. Actors dressed as characters from *Sesame Street*—Elmo and his friends—are on hand to thrill the little ones as part of "The Caribbean Adventure with Sesame Street" activities for kids 5 and under. The Kids Camp has daylong activities for children 6 to 12. Older kids can lose themselves in free, unlimited play at the Xbox 360 Game Garage interactive gaming center. Tweens and teens can groove to DJ-spun sounds (and vie for one of the four VIP cabanas) at Club Liquid.

The all-inclusive designation means you get a lot for your money: all meals and drinks; excellent watersports; winning service from a staff of nearly 800 employees; a full-service nursery with cribs, swings, rockers, and a coterie of nannies; and even a spa, the **Red Lane** (daily 8am–8pm). Gratuities are included for everything, so you don't have to worry about doling out tips all day. Note, however, that you'll pay extra for many spa treatments, certain scuba-diving courses and excursions, and international telephone calls.

Accommodations come in 12 different categories and a variety of configurations. All rooms and suites have king-size beds. The higher-category suites have four-poster beds, a "Premium Bar" and a fully stocked refrigerator based on your personal requests, and 8am-to-8pm concierge service. The luxury suites offer 24-hour butler service, with professionally trained butlers catering to your every whim. The largest unit, the French Village three-bedroom suite, can accommodate up to 11 people. The resort's newest section is the all-suites **Italian Village,** featuring a 1,115-sq.-m (12,002-sq.-ft.) pool with a giant **water park** (with wave pool) and 168 brand new family suites.

Food is available somewhere on the premises 24 hours a day, but room service is offered only in the butler-service suites. In general, the food is plentiful, if not particularly inspired. Among the 16 restaurants, you can get Italian **(Giuseppe's),** Tex-Mex **(Arizona's),** seafood **(Schooners),** or Japanese **(Kimonos).** For the kids, the very cool **Bobby D's** is a 1950s-style diner with burgers, hot dogs, and spaghetti.

Lower Bight Rd. (P.O. Box 186), Providenciales, Turks and Caicos, B.W.I. www.beaches.com. ⓒ **800/232-2437** in the U.S., or 649/946-8000. Fax 649/946-8001. 620 units. Winter $6,400–$25,000 weekly; off season $5,400–$18,000. Rates are all-inclusive. AE, DISC, MC, V. **Amenities:** 10 restaurants; 7 bars; babysitting; children's center w/pool; fitness center, basketball, volleyball; Internet cafe; 8 outdoor pools; 2 saunas; spa; 4 lit tennis courts; watersports equipment (extensive); nurses' station. In room: A/C, ceiling fan, TV, CD players, in-room bars (in concierge rooms), fridge, Wi-Fi (free).

The Gansevoort Turks + Caicos ★★ The Gansevoort brand projects effortless chic. The resorts have an ingrained urbanity—no wonder, since the line's flagship hotel is the Gansevoort in Manhattan's Meatpacking District. Trendiness aside, these are superbly run hotels that dispense a healthy sense of hospitality. The Gansevoort Turks + Caicos has the hipness quotient down, but it also has a killer Grace Bay setting, to which every one of the 91 rooms genuflects daily. The sun-blasted pool is the nerve center of the resort, dotted with personal "floating islands"—but is it just me, or does it feel a little claustrophobic at times? Rooms are brilliantly outfitted, with electric blackout blinds, LCD TVs, and cutting-edge kitchens loaded with Liebherr, Gaggenau, and Bosch appliances; play "find the fridge" (it's camouflaged in the cabinetry). Bathrooms have glass-encased rain showers. And can I say that the big, deep tubs filled from a spigot high in the ceiling make me very happy? The "wow" factor hits the roof (literally) with four

344-sq.-m (3,700-sq.-ft.) three-bedroom penthouses all boasting wraparound terraces, designer kitchens, personal concierge, and a VIP buffet. The **Restaurant & Beach Bar** is still working out the kinks in bringing a sophisticated touch to the island dining scene. But the breezy vibe is all Provo—especially at night, when the palms rustle in the trade winds and warm candlelight softens any urban edges.

Grace Bay, Providenciales, Turks and Caicos, B.W.I. www.gansevoortturks andcaicos.com. ✆ **888/844-5986** in the U.S., or 649/941-7555. Fax 309/210-9091. 91 units. Winter $650–$800 double, $950–$5,000 suite; off season $500–$650 double, $750–$3,250 suite. Rates include continental breakfast. Children 11 and under stay free in parent's room. Extra person $100 per night. AE, MC, V. **Amenities:** Restaurants; 2 bars; babysitting; children's program; concierge; fitness center; outdoor pool; room service; spa; watersports equipment (extensive). *In room:* A/C and ceiling fan, TV/DVD, CD player, kitchen (suites), kitchenettes (studios), MP3 docking station, washer/dryer (suites), Wi-Fi (free).

The Regent Grand ★   Occupying a central spot on the Grace Bay oceanfront, this all-suites resort is an impressive property of classical design, with a breathtaking centerpiece of a pool (the biggest in the TCI), a tennis court, and a shopping-and-restaurant complex next door in Regent Village. The suites are large and comfortably furnished and have everything you need (including fully equipped kitchens), though layouts are a little uninspired. But that's okay, since you'll have every amenity under the sun and a swell piece of beachfront to play on. Check the website for good-value special offers and packages.

Grace Bay Rd. (P.O. Box 124), Providenciales, Turks and Caicos, B.W.I. www. theregentgrandresort.com. ✆ **877/288-3206** in the U.S. and Canada, or 649/941-7770. Fax 649/941-7771. 54 units. Winter $489 double, $794–$1,358 1-bedroom suite, $1,058–$1,886 2-bedroom suite, $2,185–$2,875 3-bedroom suite; off season $375–$590 double, $656–$1,047 1-bedroom suite, $759–$1,541 2-bedroom suite, $1,840–$2,300 3-bedroom suite. Ask about Christmas holiday rates. Children 11 and under stay free in parent's room. Extra person $50 per night ($80 holidays). Rates include continental breakfast delivered to the suite and airport transfers. AE, MC, V. **Amenities:** 2 restaurants; 2 bars; babysitting; bikes; fitness center; pool; room service; spa; 2 lighted tennis courts; watersports equipment (extensive). *In room:* A/C, ceiling fan, TV/DVD, full kitchens, Wi-Fi (free).

Seven Stars Resort ★★ ☺   This luxury resort in the heart of Grace Bay has prevailed through financial difficulties and a changeover in ownership. Although it has given up its once-considerable expansion plans, it still has plenty to recommend it: a prime oceanfront location; spacious and beautifully appointed elegant one-, two-, and three-bedroom suites; and a palpable commitment to service. The entrance is lined with a classic colonnade of palms.

The sprawling saltwater pool is the only heated pool on the island, great for toddlers. Kids also have a large playground to romp around. The **Deck,** overlooking Grace Bay, is a fun spot to drink in the sunset and dine on a light menu. Have lunch at the alfresco **Sand Dollar,** near the pool. **Seven** is the resort's inspired main restaurant, with a full menu of Caribbean-inspired Continental fare. Rooms are decorated in crisp British-Colonial style, with large windows, marble floors, and full or galley kitchens; many have wraparound terraces and four-poster beds. I like the fact that the resort rates have become more competitive, and I like Seven Stars' community spirit: Every year at Christmas it gives Provo a holiday gift in the form of a big Christmas tree done up in glittering lights, set in the middle of the traffic roundabout that fronts the property.

Grace Bay, Providenciales, Turks and Caicos, B.W.I. www.sevenstarsresort. com. ✆ **866/570-7777** in the U.S. and Canada, or 649/941-7777. Fax 649/941-8601. 107 units. Winter $715–$990 junior suite, $825–$1,090 1-bedroom suite, $2,150 2-bedroom suite, $2,475–$3,850 3- and 4-bedroom suites; off season $515–$840 junior suite, $515–$765 1-bedroom suite, $1,550–$2,000 2-bedroom suite, $2,325–$3,700 3- and 4-bedroom suites. Extra person 12 and over $50–$100 per night. Rates include continental breakfast. AE, MC, V. **Amenities:** 2 restaurants; pool lounge; babysitting/nanny service; children's playground and kids' camp; concierge; fitness center; outdoor pool; spa; 2 lighted tennis courts; watersports equipment (extensive); Wi-Fi (free, in pool, reception, and restaurant areas). *In room:* A/C, ceiling fans, flatscreen TV, DVD and CD players, Internet (free), full kitchen (in suites), galley kitchen (in studios).

Villa Renaissance ★★ 🎁 This boutique gem lies on a central stretch of Grace Bay oceanfront. It has a lovely reception area (the Pavilion), a large gorgeous mosaic pool, and the on-site full-service **Teona Spa.** You can order room service from **Vix Bar & Grill** in the adjacent Regent Village complex. The classical architecture (much like an Italian villa) is beautiful, and the suites are nicely outfitted. All suites come with sleek, fully equipped kitchens; suites in the main villa have ocean views from Juliet balconies.

Grace Bay (P.O. Box 592), Providenciales, Turks and Caicos, B.W.I. www.villa renaissance.com. ✆ **877/285-8764** in the U.S., or 649/941-5300. Fax 649/941-5340. 32 units. Winter $725–$1,040 1-bedroom suite, $900–$1,375 2-bedroom suite, $1,850 3-bedroom suite, $2,300 penthouse; off season $535–$790 1-bedroom suite, $775–$1,000 2-bedroom suite, $1,300 3-bedroom suite, $1,600 penthouse. Extra person 13 or over $85 per night. Rates include continental breakfast. AE, DISC, MC, V. **Amenities:** Pool bar; babysitting; bikes; concierge; fitness center; room service; spa; watersports equipment. *In room:* A/C, TV/DVD, fridge, kitchen, Wi-Fi (free).

MODERATE/EXPENSIVE
The Alexandra ★ 🔥 This sunny, sprawling all-suites resort has a great location directly on Grace Bay and a big, beautiful pool with

a swim-up bar, a spa, and a fitness center. It represents good value, especially if you want to be smack-dab on Grace Bay and don't want to spend a fortune. The Alexandra has gotten a spiffy makeover, with a handsome new reception center and newly renovated suites. You can choose from studios all the way up to four-bedroom suites (lockouts) in several categories: garden, oceanview, and oceanfront. The suites are smallish but pleasantly outfitted, and all but the studios have sleek, fully equipped kitchens (studios have kitchenettes). Rooms may not approach the ultra-luxe factor of places like the Regent Palms, next door, but they're sun-filled and comfortable. The Alexandra has a lot going for it, especially the 2011 addition of **Mango Reef,** the popular restaurant that left its longtime location at the Royal Reef Resort to set up shop here in an inviting, sun-splashed beachside setting. That alone should draw more and more folks to the Alexandra's winning Grace Bay locale.

Princess Dr., Grace Bay, Providenciales, Turks and Caicos, B.W.I. www.alexandraresort.com. ✆ **800/284-0699** in the U.S., or 649/946-5807. Fax 649/946-4686. 145 units. Winter $320–$435 deluxe studio, $450–$1,650 1-bedroom suite, $675–$800 2-bedroom suite, $1,700 4-bedroom suite; off season $235–$325 deluxe studio, $325–$500 1-bedroom suite, $575–$660 2-bedroom suite, $1,420 4-bedroom suite. Children 11 and under stay free in parent's room. Ask about meal packages at Mango Reef. AE, MC, V. **Amenities:** Restaurant; grill/deck bar; swim-up bar; babysitting; concierge; fitness center; outdoor pool and kids' pool; room service; spa; 2 lighted tennis courts; volleyball; watersports equipment (extensive). *In room:* A/C, ceiling fan, TV/DVD, full kitchen (kitchenette in studios), washer/dryer (most suites), Wi-Fi (free).

Club Med Turkoise ★   Set on 28 hectares (69 acres) of sun-blasted scrubland on a white strip of beachfront overlooking Grace Bay, this adults-only all-inclusive resort was one of the pioneers of Grace Bay when it opened in 1984. To be honest, the oldest resort on the island has been showing its age for some time. The landscaping is negligible, the food serviceable at best, and from the outside the accommodations look more like a church camp than a beach resort. Amplified music kicks in around sunset, and it's certainly noisier and more hyperactive than anything else on Grace Bay. But who cares? Even in the off season, the resort is packed with happy campers, filled to capacity when other resorts are half-full. Its appeal lies in its mix of nonstop activity and communal fun. Singles and couples come here to play in the sun—and this sprawling beachside campus has plenty of toys, including a very cool flying trapeze.

The village-style cluster of basic two- and three-story accommodations contains comfortable, colorful rooms with twin or king-size beds, all designed with beachfront living in mind. The all-inclusive designation means that meals are included as well as most drinks—except champagnes, top-shelf liquors and wines, and canned and bottled drinks (sodas and juices are served by the glass). Among the three restaurants are **Grace Bay,** which serves breakfast, lunch, and dinner buffet style, and **Lucayan,** which offers a la carte meals and is open in the evening only (7:15–8:45pm; reservations required). Most meals are served at long, communal tables. The third restaurant, **Sharkie's,** is a seaside snack bar.

Grace Bay, Providenciales, Turks and Caicos, B.W.I. www.clubmed.us. © **800/258-2633** in the U.S., or 649/946-5500. Fax 649/946-5497. 290 units. Winter $1,759–$2,405 per person weekly; off season $1,556–$2,195 per person weekly. Rates are all-inclusive. AE, MC, V. No children 17 or under allowed. **Amenities:** 3 restaurants; 2 bars; open-air nightclub; basketball; flying trapeze; golf (Provo Golf Club); gym; outdoor pool; softball; 8 tennis courts (4 lit); trampoline; volleyball; watersports equipment (extensive); wellness center w/spa treatment rooms; Wi-Fi (free). *In room:* A/C, flatscreen TV, clock radio/CD player, minifridge.

Coral Gardens/Reef Residences on Grace Bay 🏷 This

Grace Bay resort fronts one of the beach's top snorkeling and diving spots on Bight Reef in the Princess Alexandra National Park. The Reef Residences lies behind Coral Gardens and has no ocean views—plus, the two places have different management teams. Most, if not all, of the units are condos, with each unit privately owned. Suites are large (full kitchens and even walk-in closets in some) and deep, with expansive balconies. Excellent snorkeling and diving opportunities lie literally right outside your door; the dive operator **Caicos Adventures** has a shop on-site and offers scuba courses, snorkeling tours, and complimentary snorkeling equipment.

Lower Bight Rd., Grace Bay (P.O. Box 281), Providenciales, Turks and Caicos, B.W.I. www.coralgardens.com. © **800/532-8536** in the U.S., or 649/941-3713. Fax 649/941-5171. 30 units. Winter $249 garden double, $399–$449 1-bedroom oceanfront suite, $499–$599 2-bedroom oceanfront suite, $559–$750 penthouse; off season $199 garden double, $300–$349 1-bedroom oceanfront suite, $400–$500 2-bedroom oceanfront suite, $459–$599 penthouse. Children 9 and under stay free in parent's room. Extra person 10 years or older $30 per night. Rates include full breakfast. AE, DISC, MC, V. **Amenities:** 1 restaurant; 1 bar; babysitting; bikes; dive and snorkel shop; fitness center; 2 outdoor pools; spa; watersports equipment (extensive). *In room:* A/C, TV, CD and DVD players, full kitchen, washer/dryer (in penthouses and Ocean Grand suites), Wi-Fi (free).

Le Vele ★ This sleek boutique property sits on a picture-perfect stretch of Grace Bay Beach. The resort contains only 22 units but is a smart option for families. Each of the one-, two-, and three-bedroom condominium suites has room to spare, with oceanfront views, wraparound balconies, and full kitchens (excluding the studio suites). If you're looking for a quiet, intimate spot with a clean design steps away from the sea, this should fit the bill. It's not for everyone: The blocky white concrete gives the place a clinical feel, and it doesn't have a restaurant or bar. But you're just minutes away from a number of fine Grace Bay dining options. Or you can take advantage of the suites' complete kitchens, with ovens, ranges, microwaves, stainless-steel fridges, and dishwashers.

Grace Bay, Providenciales, Turks and Caicos, B.W.I. www.leveleresort.com. © **888/272-4406** in the U.S., or 649/941-8800. 22 units. Winter $474 double, $664 1-bedroom suite, $949 2-bedroom suite, $1,360 3-bedroom suite; off season $348 double, $474 1-bedroom suite, $696 2-bedroom suite, $1,044 3-bedroom suite. Extra person $60 per night. Rates include continental breakfast delivered to your suite. AE, DISC, MC, V. **Amenities:** Babysitting; bikes; concierge; fitness center; infinity pool; watersports equipment. In room: A/C, TV/DVD/CD, full kitchens, washer/dryers (excluding studio suites), Wi-Fi (free).

4

Ocean Club Resorts ★ ☺ These two sprawling condo-hotel complexes are within a mile of one another, both with prime oceanfront acreage on Grace Bay. The original, **Ocean Club East,** lies across from the Provo Golf Club, spread across a 3-hectare (7½-acre) piece of landscaped property. It shares amenities with its newer sister resort, **Ocean Club West,** and a complimentary shuttle runs between the two. Both comprise a low-lying series of buildings surrounding gardens and a courtyard.

Both resorts have 86 suites, among them studio suites, junior suites, and one-, two-, and three-bedroom deluxe suites—many with ocean views and fully equipped kitchens (studios have kitchenettes only). (The main difference between East and West is that only Ocean Club East offers studio deluxe and one-bedroom beachfront suites.) Except for the studio suites (the cheapest rental), accommodations are spacious and comfortable, with large screened balconies. The decor is light, bright, and pleasant, if not particularly exciting—but on a slice of beach this delicious, who's spending time in their room?

With their large suites and fully appointed kitchens, these resorts are family-vacation favorites. Both resorts have a Kids Clubhouse, a day camp for children ages 3½ and up from 9:30am to 1pm daily.

The resorts' main restaurant, **Opus,** located at Ocean Club East in the Ocean Plaza, offers upscale Continental dining. There's also a daily shuttle-bus service for dining in the evenings and a part-time shuttle bus for daytime shopping, both for a small fee.

Grace Bay Beach (P.O. Box 240), Providenciales, Turks and Caicos, B.W.I. www.oceanclubresorts.com. © **800/457-8787** in the U.S., or 649/946-5880. Fax 649/946-5845. 186 units. Winter $289–$309 studio suite, $329–$419 junior suite, $429–$609 1-bedroom suite, $559–$729 2-bedroom suite, $849–$989 3-bedroom suite; off season $209–$219 studio suite, $239–$329 junior suite, $359–$429 1-bedroom suite, $469–$589 2-bedroom suite, $619–$739 3-bedroom suite. Call about Christmas holiday rates. Children 12 and under stay free in parent's room. Extra person $25 per night in winter; free in summer. AE, DISC, MC, V. **Amenities:** 3 restaurants (Seaside Café is in Ocean Club West); 3 bars; babysitting; bikes; concierge; convenience store; dive shop; fitness room; 3 freshwater pools; 3 lighted tennis courts; watersports equipment (extensive). *In room:* A/C, ceiling fan, TV/VCR, kitchen (kitchenettes in studios), washer/dryer (excluding studios), Wi-Fi (free).

Royal West Indies Resort ★ ☺   This is one of the most reliable condo-hotel resorts in Provo, offering family-friendly lodging and an enviable location on prime Grace Bay beachfront. The property is pillowed in manicured gardens, the centerpiece of which is a large pool enveloped in tropical foliage. It's a pretty big place, with 99 units, but the spacious suites are situated in intimate groupings of low-rise buildings spread out over the property. Guests have a choice of oceanfront, oceanview, studio, or gardenview one- and two-bedroom suites. Suites have balconies or patios and good-size kitchenettes. The interiors have been nicely refurbished with comfortable, well-maintained furnishings and good linens. Note that the Royal West Indies is next door to Club Med, so if you're staying on the resort's eastern flank, amplified disco music may waft over at times. The resort's popular poolside restaurant, Mango Reef, has moved to the Alexandria Resort. Its replacement, **Pelican Bay Restaurant & Bar** (p. 52), serves up tasty island fare like coconut shrimp and curry fish, conch, and lobster. A shuttle travels between the resort and the Graceway IGA twice a day ($20 roundtrip for one or two people).

Grace Bay (P.O. Box 482), Providenciales, Turks and Caicos, B.W.I. www.royal westindies.com. ✆ **800/332-4203** in the U.S., or 649/946-5004. Fax 649/946-5008. 99 units. Winter $310–$425 studio, $410–$625 1-bedroom suite, $560–$795 2-bedroom suite; off season $225–$345 studio, $275–$465 1-bedroom suite, $405–$545 2-bedroom suite. Children 12 and under stay free in parent's room. Extra person 13 or over $35 per night. AE, DISC, MC, V. **Amenities:** Restaurant; bar; babysitting; bikes; Jacuzzi; 2 outdoor pools; watersports equipment (extensive); Wi-Fi (free, in lobby and hot spot). *In room:* A/C, ceiling fan, TV, kitchen, washer/dryer.

The Sands at Grace Bay ★★ ☺   The Sands has long been a popular, good-value choice on Grace Bay, but a topnotch refurbishment—including the construction of an elegant freestanding lobby—has put it in another league altogether. This sprawling all-suites condo resort sits on a sweet stretch of Grace Bay Beach. Suites have been tastefully and luxuriously updated, with granite countertops, marble sinks, and fine linens. The landscaped gardens and pools are impeccably maintained—this is one well-managed property. Choose from studio, one-bedroom, two-bedroom, or three-bedroom suites—each of which is fully appointed, with screened terraces. The suites also have full kitchens (studios have kitchenettes) and washer/dryers—great for family stays. The Sands is the site of one of the island's most popular beachfront restaurants, **Hemingway's** (p. 51), and the **Spa Tropique at the Sands.**

Grace Bay, Providenciales, Turks and Caicos, B.W.I. www.thesandstc.com. *C* **877/777-2637** in the U.S., or 649/946-5199. Fax 649/946-5198. 114 units. Winter $285–$460 studio, $460–$710 1-bedroom suite, $560–$710 2-bedroom suite, $900–$1,200 3-bedroom suite; off season $185–$335 studio, $335–$535 1-bedroom suite, $435–$580 2-bedroom suite, $630–$830 3-bedroom suite. Ask about Christmas and New Year's rates. Children 11 and under stay free in parent's suite (maximum of 2). AE, DISC, MC, V. **Amenities:** Restaurant; bar; supermarket shuttle ($8 per person round-trip); babysitting; bikes; dive shop; fitness center; Jacuzzi; 3 outdoor pools; spa services; tennis court; watersports equipment (extensive). *In room:* A/C, ceiling fan, TV, full kitchen (kitchenette in studios), washer/dryer, Wi-Fi (free).

Turks & Caicos Club ★ 🎒 This quiet and peaceful Lower Bight pioneer has only 21 suites (one- and two-bedroom), each with four-poster beds, a gourmet kitchen, and its own big, private porch. You can choose from oceanfront, with gorgeous views of Grace Bay Beach, or poolside (with lower rates). The rooms are nicely appointed (kitchens have state-of-the-art KitchenAid appliances), but the porches make it special. A talented chef is on board at the in-house restaurant, **Simba ★**; the island-style conch chowder is a fiery masterpiece. Check the website for good-value special offers.

Grace Bay (P.O. Box 687), Providenciales, Turks and Caicos, B.W.I. www.turks andcaicosclub.com. *C* **877/698-2258** in the U.S. and Canada, or 649/946-5800. Fax 649/946-5858. 21 units. Winter $445–$595 1-bedroom suite, $1,095 2-bedroom suite; off season $325–$495 1-bedroom suite, $655–$845 2-bedroom suite. Rates include continental breakfast. AE, MC, V. **Amenities:** Restaurant; pool bar; fitness room; room service; watersports equipment (extensive). *In room:* A/C, TV/VCR/DVD, kitchen, MP3 speakers, Wi-Fi (free).

The West Bay Club ★★ 🏖 With a killer location and topnotch accommodations, the West Bay Club represents good value on beachfront Grace Bay. Opened in 2009, this Lower Bight property is much less frenetic than its trendy neighbor to the west, the Gansevoort. But if it's laid-back luxury you're after—as well as the services of a warm, friendly staff—this is the spot for you. The commodious suites are plenty swell: The West Bay Club has some of the biggest rooms on Grace Bay, sheathed in marble floors and outfitted with 46-inch flatscreen TVs, DVD/CD surround-sound theater systems, MP3 docks, full kitchens with stainless-steel appliances and granite countertops, oceanfront terraces, and a surplus of closet space. Particularly good value are the glamorous three- and four-bedroom suites, the largest of which are 353 sq. m (3,800 sq. ft.), with sweeping Grace Bay views. By design, the hotel amenities are modest—the pool is smallish, the restaurant has only 10 tables (but the food is fresh and delicious), and the bar is just a smattering of stools. (If you're looking for a sizzling lounge scene, just walk a few meters west to the Gansevoort.) At the West Bay Club, the emphasis is firmly on luxe rooms and a spectacular Grace Bay location. It all purrs along with the expert guidance of the warm and unpretentious management, a husband-and-wife team offering mom-and-pop luxe.

Lower Bight Rd., Grace Bay, Providenciales, Turks and Caicos, B.W.I. www. thewestbayclub.com. © **866/607-4156** in the U.S., or 649/946-8550. Fax 649/946-3722. 46 units. Winter $345 studio, $545–$682 1-bedroom suite, $715–$875 2-bedroom suite, $975 3-bedroom suite, $1,100 4-bedroom suite; off season $270 studio, $440–$600 1-bedroom suite, $630–$765 2-bedroom suite, $725 3-bedroom suite, $825 4-bedroom suite. Extra person $75 per night. Rates include European breakfast. AE, DISC, MC, V. **Amenities:** Restaurant; bar; babysitting; bikes; concierge; fitness center; kitchen provisioning; pool; room service; spa; watersports equipment. *In room:* A/C, ceiling fan, TV, DVD/CD, kitchen (except studios), MP3 docking station, washer/dryer (except studios), Wi-Fi (free).

INEXPENSIVE

Caribbean Paradise Inn 🔥 This little lodging is a real find, considering that it's only a 2-minute walk from lovely Grace Bay Beach *and* the low rates include breakfast. It has also been a hub of activity since chef Paul Newman moved the popular restaurant **Coyaba** (p. 47) to the adjoining bar/patio area; even though the restaurant is run independently from the inn, the lively dining scene gives the place a jolt of electricity. Two stories of rooms overlook the pool and lush tropical gardens. Combination bedrooms and living areas, the rooms have been nicely refreshed, each with one king-size or two full beds. Latticed balconies, tile floors, and sunny Provençal colors blunt the generic motel layout. The small bathrooms have showers only. Jean Luc Bohic is the personable owner.

Grace Bay (P.O. Box 673), Providenciales, Turks and Caicos, B.W.I. www. caribbean-paradise-inn.com. © **649/231-5020.** Fax 649/946-5022. 17 units. Winter $145–$175 double; off season $125–$165 double. Children 8 and under stay free in parent's room. Extra person $35 per night. Rates include buffet breakfast. Ask about dive packages. MC, V. **Amenities:** Bar; babysitting; outdoor freshwater pool; watersports. *In room:* A/C, ceiling fan, TV, fridge/minibar, Wi-Fi ($10/day).

Comfort Suites 🔥 This is the first franchise hotel to open on Provo, and it represents great value for its central location alone. The nicely refurbished suites are more than suitable, and the hospitality provided by the staff is exceptional. The handsomely landscaped property is a 2-minute walk to the beach, restaurants, and shops. Guests stay here in one of the spacious junior suites, with either a king-size or two double beds, or in a suite with a balcony. Accommodations are spread across two three-floor structures, enveloping a large swimming pool, pool bar, and a courtyard.

Grace Bay Rd. (P.O. Box 590), Providenciales, Turks and Caicos, B.W.I. www.comfortsuitesci.com. ✆ **888/678-3483** in the U.S., or 649/946-8888. Fax 649/946-5444. 100 units. Winter $127–$199 suite; off season $129–$169 suite. Rates include breakfast. Children 15 and under stay free in parent's room. Extra person $30 per night. AE, DISC, MC, V. **Amenities:** Bar; babysitting; outdoor pool. *In room:* A/C, TV, Wi-Fi (free).

Grace Bay Suites 🏷 Located behind Danny Buoy's restaurant off Grace Bay Road, this is a nice new entry to the budget-lodgings category. Each of its 18 studios and 6 one-bedroom suites has a patio or balcony and a small kitchenette. The complex even has a small swimming pool.

Grace Bay Rd., Providenciales, Turks and Caicos, B.W.I. http://gracebaysuites.com. ✆ **649/941-7447.** Fax 649/941-5639. 24 units. Winter $195 suite, $148 studio; off season $145 suite, $128 studio. Children 11 and under stay free in parent's room. Extra person $25 per night. AE, DISC, MC, V. On-site parking. **Amenities:** Outdoor pool. *In room:* A/C, TV, kitchenette, Wi-Fi (free).

Sibonné Beach Hotel ★ 🏷 One of the first lodgings constructed on the fabulous sands of Grace Bay Beach, this hotel is a fantastic value, as long as you don't expect a huge laundry list of resort amenities (and you don't expect the staff to shower you with love). What it does have is a laid-back, informal vibe; alluring courtyard gardens; and knockout Grace Bay views. It's considerably more charming and personable than any chain-style hotel, with comfortable rooms done up in a light, breezy decor. For a stupendous deal on Grace Bay, book the one-bedroom upstairs apartment, detached from the actual hotel. It has a full kitchen, with pots, pans, plates, the works; a separate living room; a big, comfortable bed; and two oceanfront patios, one screened, one open—you'll feel as if you have your own sunny beachfront cottage within spitting distance of the million-dollar sands of the Somerset. On-site is the **Bay Bistro,** a casual beachside restaurant offering exceptional breakfast, lunch, and dinner fare; and **Junior's Bar,** whose bartender extraordinaire, Junior Brown, is considered one of the most creative mixologists on the island. *Note:* Sibonné does not accept children 12 or under in the winter or holiday season.

Grace Bay (P.O. Box 144), Providenciales, Turks and Caicos, B.W.I. http://sibonne.com. ✆ **800/528-1905** in the U.S., or 649/946-5547. Fax 649/946-5770. 29 units. Winter $125–$235 double, $350 apt; off season $110–$205 double, $285 apt. Children 11 and under $35 (no children 12 and under in winter or holiday season). Extra person $45 per night. AE, MC, V. **Amenities:** Restaurant; bar; outdoor pool. *In room:* A/C, ceiling fan, TV, fridge, Wi-Fi (free).

Trade Winds Condotel 🐚 Another smart, affordable option lies on Grace Bay Road, a minute or two from the beach and in the heart of the Grace Bay action. Each of the 18 one-bedroom suites comes with a fully equipped modern kitchen, washer/dryer, a living-room sleeper sofa, and patios or balconies. Trade Winds also has a secluded private pool and a lushly planted barbecue area. The upper suites have ocean views.

382 Grace Bay Rd., Providenciales, Turks and Caicos, B.W.I. www.tradewinds condotel.com. ✆ **866/389-6673** in the U.S., or 649/946-5194. Fax 649/946-4029. 18 units. Winter $295–$315 suite; off season $260–$280 suite. Children 12 and under stay free in parent's room. Extra person $35 per night. AE, DC, DISC, MC, V. On-site parking. **Amenities:** Outdoor pool. *In room:* A/C, TV, kitchen, washer/dryer, Wi-Fi (free).

Northwest Point

Those in the know say that this section of Provo represents the future of the country's hospitality industry. Unlike Grace Bay's long, developable stretch of beach, the beaches at the Northwest Point are serendipitous little coves with pockets of powdery white sand and turquoise seas. The waters along the Northwest Point are part of the **Northwest Point Marine National Park,** a protected 8km-long (5-mile) reef system that features some of the world's top wall and reef diving.

Currently the Northwest Point has only two accommodations: Amanyara (see below), and the **Northwest Point Resort** condominium hotel (www.northwestpointresort.com). To reach either, you travel through the Blue Hills neighborhood, where beachfront shacks dish out fresh conch dishes, good music, and a sunny barefoot vibe (see "Head for the [Blue] Hills," in chapter 3).

Amanyara ★★★ When it opened in early 2006, the first Amanresorts property in the West Indies was such a big deal that *Travel + Leisure* magazine devoted an entire cover article to it. It's a stunning property, no question. But this is unfussy luxury, with Amanresorts' trademark purity of form, integrity of materials, and obeisance to eco-principles. The prices are heart-stopping, so it's reassuring to know that no detail has been left to chance. Classically aligned wooden buildings practically float on glassy reflecting pools. The bar has an ingenious tepee-style ceiling that soars toward the sunlight. Linen-wrapped sofa beds lord over the infinity pool, its bottom fashioned of speckled black Indonesian lava.

The 40 individual pavilions are stand-alone houses, utterly private; a few have ocean views. Wraparound patios are enveloped in native scrub brush, sea grape, and sea ox-eye daisies. It's very earthbound, all polished teak and sisal matting, except for the exceptional gadgets: Touch a button and lower the privacy screens, groove to the surround-sound Bose system, or watch the flatscreen TV as you soak in the freestanding bathtub. Or head to the breathtaking spa, which overlooks a reflection pond, for some serious pampering.

The **Restaurant** serves a menu with Asian and Mediterranean influences either inside or on a candlelit patio; the **Beach Club** serves lunch and afternoon meals. The smiling resort staff love children; management is happy to provide not only cribs and nannies but Diaper Champs, toddler stools, and training potties—the kitchen even makes homemade baby food! But it has been my experience that babies being, well, babies and typically boisterous toddlers do not a happy Amanyara clientele make—and who can blame them? Guests come here to catch up on some serious R & R.

All that peace and quiet is tied to location as well: The resort lies on the island's northwest shore, a fairly isolated spot reached by traveling a winding two-lane road some 25 minutes from the airport. If you're keen on exploring the island, know that you're a good 30- to 40-minute drive from the action in Provo.

Note that the resort has several privately owned three-, four-, and five-bedroom villas. Each villa is centered around its own infinity pool and has a personal cook and housekeeper.

P.O. Box 901, Providenciales, Turks and Caicos, B.W.I. www.amanyara.com. *℃* **866/941-8133** in the U.S., or 649/941-8133. Fax 649/941-8132. 40 private pavilions. Winter $1,650–$2,350 pavilion, $5,100 pavilion suite, $5,950–$14,600 villa; off season $1,450–$2,150 pavilion, $4,200 pavilion suite, $5,200–$13,350 villa. Ask about Christmas holiday rates. Children 11 and under stay free in parent's pavilion. Extra person $100 per night. Rates include private airport transfers, minibar (except spirits), in-room Internet access, and all telephone calls. AE, MC, V. **Amenities:** 2 restaurants; bar/lounge; afternoon tea; babysitting; boutique; fitness center; library; nature discovery center; outdoor pool; screening room; spa; 2 Har-Tru clay tennis courts; watersports equipment (extensive). *In room:* A/C, TV, DVD/CD player, minibar/fridge, Wi-Fi (free).

Turtle Cove

Turtle Cove Inn 🗝 You'll be hard-pressed to find a better lodging deal in Provo than this two-story hotel, built in a U shape around a freshwater swimming pool amid tropical vegetation. It's a longtime favorite with divers and boaters, and a good choice for vacationers on a budget (it's the well-run sister inn to Sibonné, the charming and equally well-run Grace Bay oceanfront resort). A few feet away, boats dock directly at the hotel's pier, which juts into Seller's Pond amid the many yachts floating at anchor. Each bedroom is clean and simply but adequately furnished, with views over either the pool or the marina. Turtle Cove has a number of fun, funky restaurants. Ask about weekly rates.

Turtle Cove Marina, Suzie Turn Rd. (P.O. Box 131), Providenciales, Turks and Caicos, B.W.I. www.turtlecoveinn.com. © **888/495-6077** in the U.S., or 649/946-4203. Fax 649/946-4141. 28 units. $99 double; $145 marina-view apt. (3-night minimum). Children 12 and under stay free in parent's room. AE, MC, V. **Amenities:** Restaurant; bar; babysitting; outdoor pool. *In room:* A/C, ceiling fan, TV, fridge, Wi-Fi (free).

CAICOS CAYS
Parrot Cay

Parrot Cay ★★★   This luxury resort is a favored retreat of celebrities, but you don't have to be a movie star to enjoy Parrot Cay's warm embrace and high service standards—standards that are impeccably maintained. Parrot Cay defines excellence. More importantly, our 6-year-old wants to move here. To that we say "Amen, sister!" Parrot Cay is a wonderful place to be.

The resort lies on an isolated and private 400-hectare (988-acre) island—reputedly a former pirate's lair—with a powdery white-sand beach. The compound features 10 white colonial-style buildings, each with a terra-cotta-tile roof. Rooms have louvered doors that open onto terraces or verandas, oyster-white walls with tongue-and-groove paneling, and mosquito netting over four-poster beds. The spacious tiled bathrooms are beautifully appointed with big tubs and the spa's irresistible Invigorate toiletries. The best units are the roomy, handsome beach houses and villas, which offer utter privacy and direct access to the beach, not to mention plunge pools and hardwood verandas. Beach villas (one to three bedrooms) are even roomier, with swimming pools and kitchenettes.

Many come to Parrot Cay for the sublime treatments in the **COMO Shambhala** holistic spa, the finest spa in the Caribbean: a wood pavilion wrapped in a sea of glass that looks out over the marsh wetlands. In addition, the resort has an infinity pool and access to scuba diving, Hobie Cats, snorkeling, kayaks, and water-skiing.

During the Christmas holidays and spring breaks, when families come for long stays, this celeb magnet becomes a big softie for kids; the shallow waters are seeded with colorful conch shells for kids' treasure hunts and messages in bottles appear on the beach.

The only drawback here is that your meals are limited to the resort's two restaurants, and prices are not gentle. Luckily, the food is amazingly fresh and impeccably sourced, and the bountiful breakfasts (included in the rates) are among the best in the TCI.

The **Terrace** restaurant, in the resort's main building, serves breakfast and dinner, specializing in Mediterranean cuisine. Lunch and dinner are served in **Lotus,** a romantic torch-lit poolside restaurant with Southeast Asian–inspired cuisine (along with regular-Joe lunch favorites like hamburgers); both restaurants offer a healthful Shambhala spa menu.

Parrot Cay (P.O. Box 164), Providenciales, Turks and Caicos, B.W.I. www.parrot cay.com or http://parrotcay.como.bz. Ⓒ **866/388-0036** in the U.S., or 649/946-7788. Fax 649/946-7789. 60 units. Winter $450–$900 double, $1,500 1-bedroom suite, $2,900 1-bedroom beach house, $3,500–$6,700 beach villa; off season $450–$800 double, $950–$1,200 1-bedroom suite, $2,000–$2,300 1-bedroom beach house, $2,600–$5,400 beach villa. Ask about meal plans and Christmas holiday rates. Children 11 and under stay free in parent's room (max 1 child in Terrace, Garden View, and Ocean-Facing rooms; max 2 children in 1-bedroom suites, 1-bedroom beach houses, and 1-bedroom villas). Extra person 13 and over $254 per night. Rates include full American breakfast and airport transfers by car and hotel boat (commercially scheduled flights only). AE, MC, V. Reached by a 30-min. private boat ride north from Provo, leaving from Leeward Marina. **Amenities:** 2 restaurants; 2 bars; babysitting; fitness center; Jacuzzi; nature trail; outdoor pool; room service; sauna; spa; 2 tennis courts; watersports equipment (extensive). *In room:* A/C, ceiling fan, TV/DVD, radio/CD player, kitchenette (in some), minibar, Wi-Fi (free).

Pine Cay

The Meridian Club ★★ Don't expect luxury of the marble-floors or gilded-chandeliers variety—this is what is lovingly referred to as "barefoot elegance"—and be prepared to live without television, radio, or even air-conditioning. This is the high life of an entirely different sort, the kind where you and a lucky few others are willing castaways on a private island paradise. The Meridian Club is one of the TCI pioneers, having been established on 324-hectare (800-acre) Pine Cay way back in 1973. To get here, you either take a 30-minute boat ride from Provo or fly in to the tiny island airstrip used by Meridian Club guests and the island's homeowners. The island has no cars: To get around, you either hoof it or, if you're in a hurry, tool around in an electric golf cart. The beach in front of the resort is simply extraordinary, and sand dollars float up without fail on the tawny sands of Sand Dollar Point, mere meters away. The snorkeling in the coral gardens offshore is satisfyingly good. The meals—included in the rates—are hearty, nutritious, plentiful, and insanely tasty—with an emphasis on fresh seafood. If you require still more privacy, opt for the Sand Dollar Cottage, a six-sided "hut" with a flagstone floor and lots of light from the louvered windows, set apart from the other rooms and almost directly on the beach.

It's all wonderful, and each of the nicely outfitted, comfortable rooms has a spacious bathroom, a screened-in porch, and a patio with a decadent outdoor shower. Check the resort website for the latest packages and special offers. *Note:* Children 11 and under are only allowed as guests in the months of June and July.

Pine Cay, Providenciales, Turks and Caicos, B.W.I. www.meridianclub.com. E-mail reservations to reservations@meridianclub.com. © **866/746-3229** in the U.S., or 649/946-7758. Fax 649/941-7010. 12 units. Winter $1,085–$1,160 club rooms, $1,235–$1,310 Sand Dollar Cottage; off season $800–$875 club room, $950–$1,025 Sand Dollar Cottage. Extra person $175 per night. Rates include all meals, afternoon tea, and roundtrip airport transfers by car and hotel boat; alcoholic beverages not included. AE, DISC, MC, V. Reached by a 30-min. private boat ride north from Provo, leaving from Leeward Marina. Closed Aug 1–Oct 31. **Amenities:** Restaurant; bar; bikes; commissary; outdoor pool; spa services; tennis court; watersports equipment (extensive); Wi-Fi (in computer room only; free). *In room:* Ceiling fan.

NORTH CAICOS

Rural, green, and charmingly slow-paced, North Caicos has its share of gorgeous powdery-sand beaches. In addition to villas and condos, North Caicos offers a handful of modest, moderately priced lodgings. Among them, the **Bottle Creek Lodge** closed in 2011. In addition, the completion of the unfinished **Royal Reef Resort** remained up in the air at press time.

Hollywood Beach Suites   This is a real getaway and almost feels like camping out, except you have a fully equipped suite in which to park your bones, and a kitchen (and outdoor barbecue grill) to cook the day's catch (supplied by local fishermen if you request it in advance). You can also have a local cook prepare a real island meal for you; just ask the helpful manager. Bikes, kayaks, and snorkeling equipment are available for guest use, but you may be tempted to simply daydream the hours away in a hammock on the tranquil beach just steps away from your suite.

Hollywood Beach Dr., Whitby, North Caicos, Turks and Caicos, B.W.I. www. hollywoodbeachsuites.com. © **800/551-2256** in the U.S., or 649/231-1020. Fax 702/973-6659. 4 units. Winter $325–$412 1-bedroom suite; off season $246–$312 1-bedroom suite. AE, MC, V. **Amenities:** Bikes; grill; watersports equipment. *In room:* A/C, ceiling fan, TV/DVD/VCR, fully equipped kitchens, no phones, washer/dryer, Wi-Fi (free).

Pelican Beach Hotel   This small, pleasant guesthouse feels as if it's from another era, with a pitched timbered ceiling and wood paneling; the only thing missing is the ticking of a grandfather clock. Outside, casuarina pines shade a conch-strewn beach lapped by turquoise seas. Owners Clifford and Susie Gardiner call this place the "unresort" and have created a mellow homey vibe, which Susie's delicious home cooking only serves to underscore. The rooms are plain but comfortable. You can snorkel nearby, have the

Gardiners arrange a boat excursion or island tour, or join the bird-watchers who flock here to see pink flamingos and ospreys. Or relax and enjoy the peace and quiet. As they like to say here at Pelican Beach: "Sometimes, you'll find, doing nothing is wonderful."

Pelican Beach, North Caicos, Turks and Caicos, B.W.I. www.pelicanbeach.tc. ⓒ **877/774-5486** in the U.S. and Canada, or 649/946-7112. 16 units. Nov 15–Apr 19 $165–$195 double, $390 2-bedroom suite; Apr 20–Nov 14 $125–$155 double, $250 2-bedroom suite. Extra person $45 per night. DISC, MC, V. **Amenities:** Restaurant; beach bar; bikes. *In room:* A/C, fridge.

MIDDLE CAICOS

The largest island in the TCI is also the least populated and currently offers only one lodging option. Luckily, it's pretty wonderful. Otherwise, visitors stay in rented villas. For a selection of villas, go to www.tcimall.tc/middlecaicos.

Note that Middle Caicos has no grocery stores, sundries stores, or gas stations. You will need to stock up on food, drink, and essential supplies in Provo or North Caicos. In North Caicos, you can buy limited groceries at **KJ Foods** (ⓒ 649/946-7705), in Whitby (just past Big Josh MacIntosh's bar); and beer, wine, soda, and liquor at **Liquors Plus** (ⓒ 649/946-7761) in My Dee's Mini Mall, in Bottle Creek. Both are on the main highway.

Tip: Don't forget to bring mosquito repellent, especially in rainy season.

Blue Horizon Resort ★★ This little eco-resort is one of the best-kept secrets in the TCI, offering secluded stays in charming wooden cottages in one of the region's most breathtaking spots: high on a bluff overlooking the iron-shore ridges of Dragon Cay and the sapphire waters of Mudjin Harbor. It's quite a sight—blue-tile-roofed cottages and villas pillowed in emerald-green bluffs—and plenty private; the resort sprawls over 20 hectares (50 acres) of lush vegetation. New owners have done a lovely job remodeling and refreshing the cottages, with comfortable furnishings, good bedding, and a pleasing palette—a sunny, breezy alternative to Provo's hermetic luxe. They've also ratcheted up the eco-excursion factor, with state-of-the-art kayaks and an airboat for exploring the thousands of acres of untouched saltwater flats. The resort has five spacious studio cottages and two villas, each with two bedrooms and two baths. All have fully equipped, self-catering kitchens (Sunset has a kitchenette) and panoramic views from big glass windows and patios, where the hillside breezes are seductive. Blue Horizon will arrange to have groceries delivered to your cottage before you arrive and have a small but choice stock of wine, beer, and triple-filtered water for sale. You can eat fresh-caught fish every night if you wish: Local fishermen are happy to provide the day's catch—grouper, say, or seasonal lobster—at your request (or you can catch it yourself). Blue Horizon will even fill up your car with fuel if you missed the last gas station in North Caicos. A **restaurant** being built on a scenic seaside bluff near the main house will serve lunch and dinner. Spend your days swimming in the clear sapphire seas of Dragon Cay, where colored sea glass dots the sands, or climb the secret stairway in the cliffs to a private beach below. Glide in one of the resort's Hobie MirageDrive kayaks with foot-pedal drive and explore nearby spots like the mangroves at Old Ferry Landing or Sand Dollar Beach. Or join resident fishing guide Adam Craton on a thrilling bonefishing expedition into the pristine Middle Caicos flats (see chapter 2). At night you can watch the moon rise above the bluffs as glittering cruise ships skim the horizon on their sail to Grand Turk.

Middle Caicos Island, Turks and Caicos, B.W.I. http://bhresort.com. © **649/946-6141.** Fax 649/946-6139. 7 units. Daily $250–$275 cottage, $375 villa; weekly $1,500–$1,700 cottage, $2,450 villa. MC, V. Closed Sept. **Amenities:** Concierge; grocery services; watersports equipment (extensive). *In room:* A/C (cottages only), TV, kitchen (kitchenette in Sunset), washer/dryer (in villas only), Wi-Fi (free).

THE TURKS ISLANDS: GRAND TURK & SALT CAY

I f you think Providenciales is laid-back, prepare yourself for the really relaxed worlds of Grand Turk and Salt Cay. These two islands are captivating charmers that hold rich architectural remnants of the TCI's colonial past. If you love to scuba dive or snorkel, have a thing for unspoiled beaches and sun-kissed seas, or crave a relaxed, back-to-basics departure from the sleek and chichi Provo resort scene, I highly recommend that you pay a visit to both of these islands during your time in the TCI.

5

GRAND TURK ★★★

If you're looking for a destination that combines world-class watersports, fascinating history, and a genial, small-town vibe, come to Grand Turk. You might say it's Mayberry by the Sea. Grand Turk is the capital island of the Turks and Caicos, although it is no longer the nation's financial and business hub, having lost that position to Provo. It is no longer the transportation hub either, as Provo receives 95% of the international airplane landings. Grand Turk was once one of the world's major salt producers, but the salt industry officially ended in the 1960s. Yes, the pace is sleepy: Donkeys clip-clop down the streets, and the old salinas ripple as white egrets and pink flamingos alight. But Grand Turk has charm to spare. The island is ringed in pillowy beaches and sapphire seas, and soft green bluffs top its northwest and eastern shores. The buttery heat from the tropical sun is cooled by constant easterly breezes.

Cockburn Town (*Coe*-burn) is the financial and business center of this tiny (11×3.2km/7×2-mile)

Grand Turk

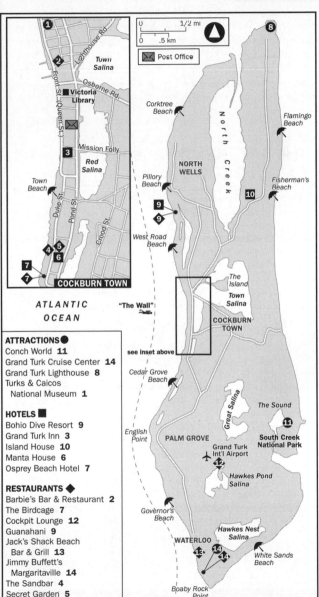

Post Office

ATLANTIC
OCEAN

"The Wall"

COCKBURN TOWN

ATTRACTIONS ●
Conch World **11**
Grand Turk Cruise Center **14**
Grand Turk Lighthouse **8**
Turks & Caicos
  National Museum **1**

HOTELS ■
Bohio Dive Resort **9**
Grand Turk Inn **3**
Island House **10**
Manta House **6**
Osprey Beach Hotel **7**

RESTAURANTS ◆
Barbie's Bar & Restaurant **2**
The Birdcage **7**
Cockpit Lounge **12**
Guanahani **9**
Jack's Shack Beach
  Bar & Grill **13**
Jimmy Buffett's
  Margaritaville **14**
The Sandbar **4**
Secret Garden **5**

island. Stroll the waterfront streets of Cockburn Town's **historic section,** particularly Duke and Front streets, home to 200-year-old structures crafted of wood and limestone. Soak up the atmosphere of the town: the vintage architecture behind picket fences entwined with crimson bougainvillea, the fragrant trees, the barefoot beachfront bars, the wet suits hanging out to dry. Stay for a couple of days, and you'll be waving to familiar faces on the street, calling the local dogs by name, and settling into your new favorite spot on Duke Street to watch the sunset over a cool Turk's Head beer.

THE DAY THE cruise ships CAME TO TOWN

Grand Turk is the kind of quirky, small-town place that lingers with you long after you've left. Maybe that's why some people were concerned that the cruise ships that started arriving at the **Grand Turk Cruise Center** in February 2006 would rend the very fabric that makes this place unique. In a 40-year land-lease deal with the TCI government, Carnival Cruise Lines built a $42-million "tourism village" designed to look like a Bermudan salt-rakers' settlement from the early 19th century. The idea that a projected half-million visitors would descend on little Grand Turk annually has been a cause for concern, but so far the cruise center at Grand Turk has been an unqualified success: In just 4 years, Grand Turk is one of the top-ranked cruise ports among cruisers. It's provided economic relief for a battered and beleaguered island still in recovery from a Category 5 hurricane and the global recession. Restaurants and businesses that cater to the cruise crowd are thriving, and local tour operators have jumped on the bandwagon with a range of shore excursions. Cruise-ship passengers aren't running wild in the streets at all hours, either. The ships usually pull in to port at daybreak and pull out by midafternoon—and many passengers never even leave the center, set far enough away from the center of Cockburn Town that the lovely, laid-back rhythms of Grand Turk continue apace. That may change, however, when the **Carnival Welcome Center,** occupying a full block on Front Street, is completed in late 2012. Like the Grand Turk Cruise Center, the Welcome Center will be a big shopping plaza, and cruise-ship passengers can arrive here by water taxi.

For more on the cruise center, see "Exploring the Island," below.

Essentials

The **Turks & Caicos Tourist Board** has an office in Grand Turk (Front St., Cockburn Town; www.turksandcaicostourism.com; ℂ **649/946-2321**). Office hours are Monday to Friday from 8:30am to 4:30pm.

For information on getting to Grand Turk from Providenciales, as well as information about getting around the island, see "Grand Turk: Getting There & Getting Around," in chapter 6.

[FastFACTS] GRAND TURK

Area Code   The area/country code for the TCI is **649.**

ATMs & ABMs   **FirstCaribbean** has 24-hour ABM service at its main branch on Grand Turk. **Scotiabank** has a 24-hour ATM at Waterloo Plaza on Grand Turk.

Banks   Branches and ATMs of **FirstCaribbean International Bank** (www.firstcaribbeanbank.com; ℂ **649/946-4245**) and **Scotiabank** (www.scotiabank.com; ℂ **649/946-4750**) are at convenient and central locations on Grand Turk.

Emergencies   Call ℂ **649/946-2299** if you need the police.

Hospitals & Medical Facilities   The **Cockburn Town Medical Centre** (ℂ **649/941-2900**) is the Grand Turk branch of the **Turks & Caicos Island Hospital,** staffed and operated by InterHealth Canada.

Internet Access   You can access the Internet at most hotels and resorts.

Language   The official language is English.

Post Office   The Grand Turk Post Office (ℂ **649/946-1334**) is located in Cockburn Town. It's open Monday to Friday from 8am to 4pm.

Restrooms   Public restrooms are located behind the public library on Front Street.

Taxes   There is a departure tax of $35, payable when you leave the islands (it's often included in the cost of your airfare). The government collects an 11% occupancy tax, applicable to all hotels, guesthouses, and restaurants in the 40-island chain. Resorts often add a 10% to 15% service charge on top of the government tax.

Scuba Diving & Snorkeling ★★★

Grand Turk's terrain is largely arid and wind-swept, but just off-shore lies some of the lushest marine real estate in the world. Many consider Grand Turk to have the finest **scuba diving** in the archipelago—in fact, a breathtakingly short .8 to 1.6km (½–1 mile) offshore (a 5- to 10-min. boat ride away). The site of most of the action is the **"Wall,"** where the western edges of the island (and its necklace of coral reef) plunge dramatically 2,134m (7,000 ft.)

into the sea—or rather the leeward side of the Turks Island Passage (aka the Columbus Passage), which lies between the Turks islands and the Caicos islands. As shown in 3-D reproductions in the **Turks & Caicos National Museum** (p. 92), the Turks and Caicos Islands are actually the flat tops of two giant plateaus. Severe underwater landslides caused portions of the plateau to collapse into the Atlantic, and thus the Wall was formed.

Scuba divers flock here to enjoy panoramic wall dives on the vertical sides of the reefs. The diving sites of the Wall have colorful names like Coral Garden, the Aquarium, the Library, and even McDonald's (so named for its coral arch). Near Governor's Beach (and just onshore from the governor's mansion at Waterloo) is a site called Chief Ministers. You'll see all manner of marine life, from giant manta rays and Nassau groupers to big, voluptuous formations of coral and sponges. You'll even spy humpback whales as they migrate south through the Turks Island Passage in the winter and early spring.

"See" is the operative word in Grand Turk diving: The visibility can exceed 30m (100 ft.). And you don't have to go deep to encounter impressive marine life: Active reef zones begin here at depths of just 9m (30 ft.), meaning you'll enjoy productive dives in better light and using better air production. The proximity of great diving to the docks also means you don't have to spend hours getting to and from your dives—after an afternoon dive you can be back on land in plenty of time for happy hour.

You can also enjoy one of the underwater world's great experiences: a **night dive** on the Wall, where, due to bioluminescence, the colors of the day become the phosphorescent illumination of the night.

When seas are calm, you can **snorkel** right off many Grand Turk beaches, including **Governor's Beach, White Sands Beach,** and **Pillory Beach** (in front of the Bohio Dive Resort). Many dive operators offer snorkeling trips out to the reef or Salt Cay or, when space allows, take snorkelers out on dive boats, where you will snorkel in water depths of approximately 8m (25 ft.). The dive shops discussed below all rent snorkel gear.

One popular snorkeling trip is to uninhabited **Gibbs Cay,** where the clear turquoise shallows are populated by docile stingrays. The stingrays are used to being fed (though please don't feed them! See "Please Don't Feed the Stingrays," below), which means they're tame enough to nudge your legs gently with their velvety wings as they glide by. It's an odd—and oddly reassuring—sensation as they float over and make contact.

Day trips to the uninhabited island of Gibbs Cay are popular, as much for the dazzling snorkeling as for the interactions with wild resident stingrays. Contrary to practices elsewhere (notably Stingray City in Grand Cayman), feeding stingrays is discouraged by the area's tour operators. As Audrey Harrell of Blue Water Divers explains, feeding fish and stingrays—or any marine life for that matter—alters their behavior and diet and makes the animals more vulnerable to environmental threats. "Stingrays conditioned to being fed can't distinguish between the motor of a tourist boat and a fishing boat," Harrell says. There's also the real potential for injury to both ray and human. According to Harrell, picking up and "petting" the stingrays rubs the protective coating off their skin, and people put themselves at serious risk "doing silly things like kissing the barb of the stingray for good luck."

Exploring the Island

People mainly travel to Grand Turk to swim, snorkel, dive, and do nothing but soak up the sun. But now that the cruise ships have arrived, local tour operators are offering a mind-numbing assortment of new activities and tours, including horseback-riding trips, jeep safaris, kayaking trips, and dune-buggy tours.

It's a pleasant bike ride to the Northwest Point to see the cast-iron **Grand Turk Lighthouse,** which was brought in pieces from the United Kingdom, where it had been constructed in 1852. Its old lens is on display in the **Turks & Caicos National Museum** (p. 92).

Conch World THEME PARK/FARM/TOUR   Opened in 2009, this combination theme park, commercial conch farm, and educational complex is located in what was described by one local as a "way-off-the-beaten-path" spot along bumpy dirt roads; the only signage is an arrow pointing the way. Conch World is generally only open when cruise ships are in port. It features a video on the history of the conch in the TCI; some 200 onshore holding tanks containing juvenile conch of different ages; and the full-grown conchs Sally and Jerry. The complex also includes the Pink Pearl Gift Shop and the Bare Naked Conch Cafe.

South Creek Sound. ✆ **649/946-1228.** Tour $17.

Grand Turk Cruise Center CRUISE CENTER   Grand Turk's inaugural season as a Caribbean cruise-ship destination saw some 136 cruise ships and 300,000 passengers arrive on the island. By 2011 those numbers had jumped to 300 port calls and 640,000 cruise passengers. The 5.7-hectare (14-acre) cruise-ship terminal is a fair distance away from the heart of Cockburn Town. The terminal was designed by the folks at Carnival Cruise Lines to resemble a colorful Bermudan-style village out of the early 19th century, much like Cockburn Town might have looked at that time. The center is planted right on the soft white sands of Governor's Beach, with hundreds of deck chairs lining the beach, a huge Jimmy Buffet's Margaritaville (see below), and the island's largest concentration of shops. It all lies mute and still until the arrival of a 3,000-passenger ship, which appears on the flat horizon just as the sun comes up—a modest speck that gets bigger and bigger as it chugalugs to shore. Cruise passengers can stay put for the duration of their visit (generally morning to mid-afternoon) or tour the island any number of ways: by red-and-white trolley train, beach buggy, Segway, or on a safari tour. Or they can participate in one of many shore excursions (scuba diving, snorkeling, horseback riding in the surf).

The cruise center is open only on days when ships come in (4–7 days a week). For non-cruisers, it's the best place on the island to shop, and it's free (and fun) to have your photo taken on the plaza with a full-size John Glenn in complete NASA spacesuit attire—part of the exhibit "Splashdown at Grand Turk," which opened in 2011, commemorating John Glenn's historic 1962 splashdown in the local waters. At press time, a new $3-million **Welcome Center** was being constructed on historic Front Street in Cockburn Town. Funded by Carnival, the cluster of buildings covers an entire city block and will contain shops, a restaurant/bar, and a tourist information service.

Waterloo Rd. www.grandturkcc.com. ✆ **649/946-1040.**

Turks & Caicos National Museum ★★ MUSEUM   The country's first (and only) museum occupies a 180-year-old residence, Guinep House, built by Bermudan wreckers from salvaged timbers. It's an unpolished old building, with creaky stairs and uneven floors. But this modest little museum is a gem. It's worth a couple of hours of your time, at least, to comb a collection that includes messages in a bottle; a 1,000-year-old **Lucayan Duho** (chieftain's chair); **Taino beads and tools;** and a **Lucayan paddle,** found in Grand Turk's North Creek, from A.D. 1100. The paddle was crafted from the native citrus wood *Rutacaae* and only survived because it was covered by a layer of mangrove peat.

GRAND TURK dive shops: MASTER LIST

The owners and operators of the following dive companies are all well-versed in diving on the island, and they know where to find marine life. They work with novices—offering good beginning courses and training—as well as experienced divers of all skill levels. Rates below are per person.

o **Blue Water Divers** (http://grandturkscuba.com; ℂ/fax **649/946-1226**): This full-service dive shop offers snorkel dives, PADI instruction, and dive packages, and even runs trips to Gibbs Cay and Salt Cay. These people are top-rate and will tell you many facts and legends about diving in their country (like the fact that the highest mountain in the Turks and Caicos is 2,400m/7,872 ft. tall, but only the top 42m/138 ft. are above sea level!). You'll save big if you buy multiday dive packages; see the website for package rates. Otherwise, a single-tank afternoon dive costs $80 to $90, with a two-tank day dive going for $85 to $95. A snorkel trip that includes a stop at Gibbs Cay costs $65 per person. Blue Water also offers full PADI certification; see their website for rates. (Mitch Rolling, the Blue Water Divers divemaster, is also the guitarist who plays at the Osprey Beach Hotel on Sun and Wed barbecue nights with the ripsaw band High Tide; see "Rippin' Ripsaw," below.)

o **Grand Turk Diving** (www.gtdiving.com; ℂ **649/946-1559**): Grand Turk native Smitty Smith is the expert instructor and guide with Grand Turk Diving, which offers complete dive/lodging packages, a resort course ($150; equipment included), and full scuba certification ($450; equipment included). Two single-tank morning dives cost $90.

o **Oasis Divers** (www.oasisdivers.com; ℂ **649/946-1128**): This dive shop offers complete divemaster services, with dive adventures along the Wall, night dives, trips to Gibbs Cay, snorkeling trips, trips to Salt Cay, and dive/accommodations packages. It does a number of dive packages with the local resorts. A morning two-tank (nonpackage) dive costs $90, a night dive is $60, an instruction course and dive from your resort is $110, and a snorkeling trip to Gibbs Cay is $55.

RAKING & MAKING salt

The large, shallow, stone-bordered ponds in the middle of Grand Turk and Salt Cay are not just nesting sites for flamingos and other brilliant birds: They are **salinas,** abandoned artifacts of the salt industry, which ruled the Grand Turk and Salt Cay economies for 300 years. The salt industry began with seasonal salt-rakers coming to the TCI from Bermuda in the late 1600s and lasted until commercial exploitation of the salinas ended in the 1960s. Grand Turk and Salt Cay, the original salt-producing islands, have several natural, shallow, inland depressions (salinas) that filled with salt water directly from the sea or percolated up from underlying rock. Bermudans improved the natural salinas, making them into rock-bordered salt pans or ponds. Salt was made by letting seawater into the salinas through sluice gates located at the beach. Water was concentrated by evaporation in one pond, then concentrated again in a second. The slushy brine was then let into smaller drying pans, where the salt crystallized. The cycle took about 90 days from start to finish, but "crops" for each set of pans were spaced by the individual stages into 20- to 30-day periods. Workers raked the crystallized salt into piles and shoveled it into wheelbarrows. Raking salt under the midday sun is an incredibly labor-intensive business, and many who worked the salt (including slaves) were felled by the brutal conditions.

Who used all this salt? From the time of the first European settlements in North America to the middle of the 1800s, salt was a critical food-preservation item. The United States was dependent on salt imports to some degree until almost the end of the 19th century. The relative importance of the Turks islands, however, dwindled as the demand for salt expanded. Dwarfed by the demand and other producers and unable to expand pond acreage, mechanize loading, or achieve economies of scale, the salt industry in the Turks islands finally collapsed in the 1960s after 300 years of production.

—Courtesy of the Turks & Caicos National Museum

Today about half of the museum's display areas are devoted to the remains of the most complete archaeological excavation ever performed in the West Indies, the wreck of a Spanish caravel (sailing ship) that sank in shallow water sometime before 1513. Used to transport local Lucayans who had been enslaved, the boat was designed solely for exploration purposes and is similar to vessels built in Spain and Portugal during the 1400s.

Treasure hunters found the wreck and announced that it was Columbus's *Pinta* in order to attract financial backers for their salvage—to guarantee a value to the otherwise valueless iron artifacts, in case there proved to be no gold onboard. There is no proof, however, that the *Pinta* ever came back to the New World after returning to Spain from the first voyage. Today the remains are referred to simply as the **Wreck of Molasses Reef.**

Although only 2% of the ship's hull remains intact, the museum exhibits contain a rich legacy of the everyday objects used by the crews and officers: an elegant copper candle holder, a miniature flagon made of pewter, a wrought-iron breech-loading swivel gun, and a pair of scissors.

Note that while opening hours change seasonally, the museum is always open on days when cruise ships are in town; schedules are available at island resorts and inns.

Guinep House, Front St., Cockburn Town, Grand Turk. http://tcmuseum.org. *C* **649/946-2160.** Admission $5 nonresidents, free for full-time island residents. Tues, Thurs–Sat 9am–1pm; Wed 1–5pm.

Shopping

The **Grand Turk Cruise Center** (www.grandturkcc.com) is the island's main shopping center, that is, until the new **Welcome Center** opens on Front Street in downtown Cockburn Town. The cruise center has a Dufry duty-free shop selling everything from souvenir caps to rum to chocolate, a Ron Jon surf shop, art galleries, jewelry stores, and souvenir shops. When the cruise ships are in town, a **flea market** is open on Front Street near the public library, selling beachwear, Haitian art, and island tchotchkes. Keep in mind that shop hours vary, and many established shops close altogether in the off season. Most shops in Cockburn Town close for lunch.

Dizzy Donkey ★ This locally owned clothing shop at the Cruise Center is carefully curated, with a smart sampling of well-priced beachwear (including Brazilian Havaianas) and a collection of TCI-made goods, including handmade sea-glass jewelry. It also sells Potcake Foundation merchandise to help raise monies for the "potcake" dogs who live on the islands (see chapter 6): bags, caps, T-shirts, aprons, even potcake-themed calendars.

Grand Turk Cruise Center. *C* **649/232-1439.**

Kalee Boutique ★ Step inside the beautifully restored 150-year-old Grand Turk Inn to this ultra-feminine boutique selling swimwear, flowing dresses, silky kurtas, sparkling jewelry, shoes, bags, and a collection of fine linens. You can buy the Salt Cay lineup of salt products here, including Fleur de Sel and bath salts.

Grand Turk Inn, Front St., Cockburn Town. *C*/fax **649/946-2827.**

Turks & Caicos National Museum Gift Shop ★★   The little gift shop of the National Museum store is packed with TCI-centric treasures, such as a collection of children's books set on Grand Turk. Look for straw hats and baskets from Middle Caicos; seaglass jewelry from glass found on Grand Turk beaches; locally roasted gourmet coffee; Salt Cay salt and bath salts; and vintage postcards, prints, and cookbooks. You can also pick up brochures for self-guided (walking or driving) birding tours, which follow trail markers fashioned from telephone poles downed in Hurricane Ike.

Turks & Caicos National Museum, Guinep House, Front St., Cockburn Town, Grand Turk. http://tcmuseum.org. ℂ **649/946-2160.**

Entertainment & Nightlife

At the previously recommended **Osprey Beach Hotel,** on Duke Street (ℂ **649/946-2666**), Wednesday and Sunday barbecues feature music by Mitch Rolling and the High Tide (see below).

Where to Eat

Barbie's Bar & Restaurant (ℂ **649/946-2981**), on Front Street, is a casual joint serving island favorites such as cracked conch, fried fish, and conch fritters.

You may not want to kill time at the Grand Turk airport—but given certain airlines' island-time mentality, you may be forced to. There's a silver lining, however: the airport restaurant. The **Cockpit Lounge** has surprisingly good island food (it feeds a lot of officials traveling to and from Cockburn Town), including shrimp and fries, lobster salad, and conch and fries, as well as sandwiches, burgers, and salads (ℂ **649/946-1095;** Mon–Sat 6am–9pm, Sun 6am–8:30pm; daily specials $11–$20). The restaurant also offers complimentary Internet access.

The Birdcage ★ CARIBBEAN/CONTINENTAL   The food is good and hearty here at the Birdcage, and the setting is pretty swell: a breezy seaside terrace around a lighted pool. The conch chowder is solid, as are the fresh fish and grilled lobster. Don't miss the **Wednesday-** and **Sunday-night poolside barbecues** here (see "Rippin' Ripsaw," above).

In the Osprey Beach Hotel. 1 Duke St., Grand Turk. http://ospreybeachhotel. com. ℂ **649/946-2666.** Main courses $16–$35. AE, MC, V. Open for breakfast, lunch, and dinner; call for hours.

Guanahani ★★ CARIBBEAN/INTERNATIONAL   This is Grand Turk's finest restaurant, with South African chef Jorika Mhende comfortably at the helm. Overlooking Pillory Beach, the space is both warm and elegant, with chocolate rattan chairs set against mint-green walls, adobe tile floors, and a wood plank ceiling.

RIPPIN' ripsaw

Hit the poolside barbecue at the **Osprey Beach Hotel** (p. 101), held every Sunday and Wednesday night, and you'll find yourself enjoying more than the excellent buffet of local dishes. Mitch Rolling and the High Tide play music with a uniquely infectious beat to which you can't help but tap your toes (or even, with the encouragement of a few Turk's Head lagers, get up and dance). That beat comes partly from the goatskin drum and maracas being played alongside the guitar-strumming Mitch (divemaster for the Blue Water Divers outfit by day); but the sound that crawls right into your nervous system comes from the guy holding that strange but familiar-looking piece of metal against his thigh and drawing another familiar-looking implement across it. He's playing a handsaw by scraping its teeth vigorously with the shaft of a long-handled screwdriver (the blade of an old knife can also be used). The result is a wonderful, rasping sound that turns any song, from a pop standard to traditional island music, into a rocking, calypso-style dance tune.

Ripsaw music, also known as "rake and scrape," is the national music of the Turks and Caicos, and it can be heard across the archipelago. Playing a ripsaw is harder than it looks. Neophytes find their arms and wrists tiring after just a few minutes, but with practice, ripsaw players learn to sustain their art for a full 2- or 3-hour show. The origins of ripsaw are unclear. Some say the art form was brought back to the islands by Belongers who fell in love with a similar style of music played in Haiti and the Dominican Republic and used locally available tools to re-create the rhythms here. Others surmise that the instrumental style was brought here by slaves of Loyalists fleeing the American Revolution. Whatever its roots, it's a style you're sure to fall in love with, too.

Feel the sea breezes through open windows as you start your meal with samosas filled with potatoes and peas or sea mushrooms stuffed with shrimp and drizzled with garlic butter. Entrees include five-spice duck breast with merlot and honeyjus, fiery peri-peri chicken, or flame-grilled ribs. Or go lobster all the way with the lobster dinner menu, which includes the chef's deft (lobster) version of Angels on Horseback.

Front St. www.bohioresort.com. ✆ **649/946-2135.** Main courses dinner $16–$35; lunch $10–$18. AE, DISC, MC, V. Daily 11am–4pm and 6–9:30pm.

Jack's Shack Beach Bar & Grill CARIBBEAN   Even though it's only open when the cruise ships are in port, Jack's is a fun spot to spend a beach day. It's located in the old South Base government complex just north of the Grand Turk Cruise Center, with lounge chairs, a volleyball net, tantalizing barbecue scents, spine-stiffening rum drinks, and a companionable island vibe. The chef serves up tasty jerk chicken, burgers, and peas 'n' rice.

South Base (500m/1,640 ft. north of the cruise center). www.jacksshack.tc. ℂ **649/232-0099.** Main courses $5–$8. MC, V. Open only when cruise ships are in (7am–7pm).

The Sandbar ★ CARIBBEAN/BURGERS   This open-air, barefoot watering hole is built right over the beach. It's a social hub for locals and visitors alike and a dog or two lying in the cool sand. The Sandbar is owned by the same two friendly Canadian sisters who run the **Manta House** across the street, and the fresh, flavorful food is not that of your typical beach bar. The shrimp and avocado salad has snap and color; equally good are curry chicken, cracked conch, grilled grouper, and Sandbar burgers.

Duke St. ℂ **649/946-1111.** Main courses $8–$16. MC, V (cash preferred). Sun–Fri noon–late (food served noon–3pm and 6–9pm).

Secret Garden ★ SEAFOOD/CARIBBEAN   Tucked in the covered backyard garden of the Salt Raker Inn, this casual eatery is a local favorite. Flattened by Hurricane Ike, it's been rebuilt (this time with concrete underpinnings), but still has a dreamy tropical-garden feel and the same reliable kitchen. Lunch specials are tasty and include grouper sandwich, barbecued chicken, and even a hearty spaghetti Bolognese. In the evening you can start with conch bites and settle on an entree of grouper, garlic shrimp, or cracked conch. On Saturday and Sunday you can order Secret

---

📎 Dining in Margaritaville

Jimmy Buffett's Margaritaville in the Grand Turk Cruise Center is an impressive sight, and for good reason: It's the largest stand-alone Margaritaville in the entire Caribbean. Its 1486 sq. m (16,000 sq. ft.) can feed up to 500 folks. The colorful, Bermudan-style restaurant is bordered by a large, lagoonlike pool with a swim-up bar, slide, and infinity edge. For a few extra bucks, you can surf or bodyboard Margaritaville's **Grand Turk Flow-Rider** ($29/hour). (Or just grab a boogie board and hit the water at Governor's Beach for free.) Margaritaville is open only on days when ships come in (4–7 days a week). Contact the cruise center at ℂ **649/946-1040** for information about restaurant hours and opening times.

Garden's famous peas 'n' grits (made here with red beans) with pigtails and conch. The Secret Garden rocks on Friday nights with the music of Mitch Rolling and his rake and scrape band.

12 Duke St. ✆ **649/946-2260.** Reservations recommended in winter. Main courses $14–$19; lobster $28. MC, V (min. $25). Tues–Sun 10:30am–2:30pm and 6–9:30pm.

Where to Stay
HOTELS, RESORTS & INNS

Most hotels add a 10% to 15% service charge, plus an 11% government occupancy tax, to the rates quoted below. Also keep in mind that many of the following resorts have a minimum-stay requirement during the winter high season.

Bohio Dive Resort ★   This resort enjoys a splendid location on beautiful Pillory Beach, the very spot where some historians believe Christopher Columbus first made landfall during his 1492 voyage to the New World. The warm, welcoming Bohio often feels like the heart of the action on Grand Turk, with big glass windows looking onto the beach and a palm-fringed wooden deck for sunny outdoor drinking and eating. The hotel's in-house dive operation, with on-site PADI instructors and divemasters, is topnotch. Each of the 12 rooms and 4 suites, located in a separate building from the main section of the resort, has its own balcony with sea views; the suites have kitchenettes. The superb resort restaurant, **Guanahani** (see above) serves breakfast, lunch, and dinner daily. Or sip a specialty Bohio cocktail at the convivial **Ike and Donkey Beach Bar,** built on the site of the original dive shack, which was blown away by Hurricane Ike in 2008. The hotel offers 3- to 7-night dive/stay packages; check the website for the latest rates.

Front St. (P.O. Box 179), Grand Turk, Turks and Caicos, B.W.I. www.bohio
resort.com. © **649/946-2135.** Fax 649/946-1536. 16 units. Winter $190
double, $225 suite; off season $165 double, $195 suite. Children 16 and
under stay free in parent's room. Extra person $30 per night. AE, MC, V.
Amenities: Restaurant; bar; bikes; dive instructors and dive shack; excursions; outdoor pool; watersports equipment. *In room:* A/C, ceiling fan, TV,
fridge (in doubles), hair dryer, kitchenette (in suites), Wi-Fi (free).

Grand Turk Inn ★★ The best accommodations in Grand Turk
would be a treasure anywhere. Sisters Katrina Birt and the late
Sandy Erb, veterans of the Key West inn scene, discovered the
old-fashioned charms of Grand Turk and the excellent bones of
this handsome Bermudan-style 150-year-old former Methodist
manse, which they lovingly renovated. The five oceanfront suites
are spacious and ultra-comfortable, with wood floors and king- or
queen-size beds dressed in smart linens; all have charming full
kitchens and private baths. The second-floor Pelican Suite can
sleep up to four people, and the two-room Flamingo Suite has
direct access to the big upper-floor sun deck—with breathtaking
views of the sea and humpback whales drifting by in winter. Relax
on the deck at night beneath a canopy of stars and stare at that
immense blue-black sea. The separate Conch Cottage has high
ceilings, tile floors, and lots of privacy. Note that the inn is just
across the street from the seawall, and when the seas are up, you
can actually feel the *booms!* reverberating from the crashing waves.
It's a phenomenon felt by every business along the Front Street
seawall.

Front St. (P.O. Box 9), Grand Turk, Turks and Caicos, B.W.I. www.grandturkinn.
com. ©/fax **649/946-2827.** 5 units. Winter $300 double; $200 off season.
Rates include continental breakfast. AE, DISC, MC, V. No children 15 or
under. **Amenities:** Bikes; snorkel equipment. *In room:* A/C, ceiling fan, TV/
DVD, hair dryer, kitchen, Wi-Fi (free).

Island House On a breezy bluff overlooking North Creek, this
inn was the creation of the late Colin Brooker, a charming English
expat, and his Grand Turk–born wife, Lucy. The inn has undergone
major renovations since Hurricane Ike, with an architectural style
that evokes the Mediterranean and rooms opening onto water
views. The five one-bedroom suites and three studios have been
handsomely furnished; all have full kitchens and balconies with
glorious views overlooking North Creek and the landscaped
grounds. It's not on the beach, but you can easily get there using
one of the vehicles available for guests to borrow. The freshwater
pool is pillowed in tropical vegetation—it's a beautiful spot to relax
at the end of the day. The hotel staff is happy to arrange any number of outdoor activities, such as diving or snorkeling, kayaking,
horseback riding, and fishing.

Lighthouse Rd. (P.O. Box 36), Grand Turk, Turks and Caicos, B.W.I. www.
islandhouse-tci.com. ✆ **649/946-1519.** Fax 649/946-1388. 8 units. Suites:
Winter (2-night package) $240 double nondiver, $315 double diver; off season (2-night package) $224 double nondiver, $299 double diver. Studios:
Winter (2-night package) $208 double nondiver, $283 double diver; off season $190 double nondiver, $265 double diver. Dive rates include 2 morning
boat dives. Children 11 and under stay free in parent's room. Rates include
personal use of vehicle and round-trip airport transfers on stays of 4 nights or
more. AE, MC, V. **Amenities:** Babysitting; bikes; outdoor freshwater pool;
watersports equipment (extensive). *In room:* A/C, ceiling fan, TV, hair dryer,
fully equipped kitchen, Wi-Fi (free).

Manta House ★   You can't ask for a better location than that
enjoyed by this little clapboard B&B, a favorite of divers. It's on
Duke Street, wrapped in a white picket fence, just meters from the
big blue sea. It's run by two vivacious and radiant Australian sisters,
Tonya and Katya, who also operate the popular Sandbar restaurant
across the street. The entire B&B has been beautifully refurbished,
and the three suites have spiffy new bathrooms, private decks, and
a soft beige/cream palette. The North Bungalow, with two bedrooms and two bathrooms, has a full kitchen and two private
patios. The Jungle Bungalow is a one-bedroom, one bathroom suite
with its own living room and private patios. The Middle Bungalow
is a three-bedroom suite with a full kitchen, a living room, and two
full baths.

Duke St. (P.O. Box 222), Grand Turk, Turks and Caicos, B.W.I. www.grandturk-
mantahouse.com. ✆ **649/946-1111.** 3 units. Weekly rates: winter $1,500
Jungle Bungalow, $1,500 North Bungalow, $1,700 Middle Bungalow; off
season $995 Jungle Bungalow, $1,300 North Bungalow, $1,500 Middle Bun-
galow. Dive packages $75 per person per day. MC, V. **Amenities:** Dive pack-
ages. *In room:* A/C, TV, kitchen (in North Bungalow and the Guesthouse).

Osprey Beach Hotel 🐦   This landmark hotel has a lovely setting on a white-sand beach where you can swim and snorkel.
Twenty-seven refurbished rooms occupy modern two-story town
houses, each with oceanfront verandas; 10 spacious units are
located across the street in the Atrium. All of the Queen suites
have full kitchens; the rest have kitchenettes or minifridges.
Rooms on the upper floors are larger and have higher ceilings, and
many have lovely, unobstructed views of the turquoise sea. The
lower rooms have direct access to the beach. Breakfast, lunch, and
dinner are served at the **Birdcage** (see above) on a seafront terrace
around the pool; tucked into a corner is the popular **Birdcage
Bar.** On Sunday and Wednesday nights, the whole of Duke Street
and beyond congregates for the **poolside barbecue buffet**
($14–$30) and the toe-tapping ripsaw music of "divemaster trou-
badour" Mitch Rolling and the High Tide.

1 Duke St. (P.O. Box 216), Grand Turk, Turks and Caicos, B.W.I. http://osprey beachhotel.com. © **649/946-2666.** Fax 649/946-2817. 37 units. Winter $175–$225 double, $100–$135 courtyard rooms (in Atrium); off season $165–$210 double, $90–$120 courtyard rooms (in Atrium). Children 16 and under stay free in parent's room. Extra person $30 per day. Dive/hotel packages available. AE, MC, V. **Amenities:** Restaurant; bar; outdoor pool; watersports equipment. *In room:* A/C, ceiling fan, TV, kitchen or kitchenette w/mini-fridges, Wi-Fi (free).

SALT CAY ★★★

When they *really* want to relax, the stressed-out denizens of Grand Turk head to sleepy Salt Cay, for a sundowner, perhaps, at the Coral Reef Bar & Grill, where you might spy a humpback whale from your barstool perch. As one Grand Turker put it, "Salt Cay has two speeds: slow and stop."

Blessedly detached from the jangly scrum of 21st-century civilization, Salt Cay, like Grand Turk, is a soulful place, littered with the ghosts of a rich and tangled past. Residents have included Taino Indians, pirates, African slaves, and the British Loyalists who brought slaves here to work the salt trade in the early 1800s. In its heyday, this 2.6-sq.-km (1-sq.-mile) island was the little engine providing much of the world's salt, and its population swelled to 1,000 citizens—a number that has slowly dwindled to 61 full-timers.

Today Salt Cay is populated by the descendants of slaves and a handful of expats, Haitian workers and a smattering of Filipino chefs and divemasters, 50 free-roaming donkeys, and even more cows. It has three grocery stores, six churches, and one charming wooden schoolhouse that is in danger of being shuttered, a sacrilege on a place proudly known as the Island of Teachers.

Salt Cay's slogan is "The Land that Time Forgot," and if you arrive by air, you'll get the idea. Civilization seems far, far away as you take in the lay of the land on the fly-in: the tiny, rural landscape dotted with abandoned salinas and old windmills, sunbaked remnants of the Bermudan salt-rakers' heyday on the island 200 years ago. Donkeys amble down dirt roads, and the one-room airport looks like a Wild West storefront, complete with hitching posts. It's a wonder you don't head home on the next flight out.

But don't. Give this, the southernmost cay of the Turks islands, a couple of days, at the very least. Grab a snorkel and mask and dip into the sparkling sea beneath the northwest bluff. Have a lively lunch at Island Thyme restaurant and gaze at the Haitian art papering the walls. Find a message in a bottle. Swim with whales. Or just take a stroll on a deserted beach and give in to the languid rhythms of one of the most spellbinding places you'll ever visit.

Salt Cay

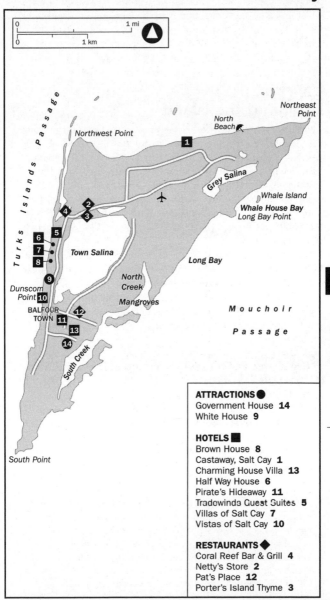

ATTRACTIONS ●
Government House **14**
White House **9**

HOTELS ■
Brown House **8**
Castaway, Salt Cay **1**
Charming House Villa **13**
Half Way House **6**
Pirate's Hideaway **11**
Tradewinds Guest Suites **5**
Villas of Salt Cay **7**
Vistas of Salt Cay **10**

RESTAURANTS ◆
Coral Reef Bar & Grill **4**
Netty's Store **2**
Pat's Place **12**
Porter's Island Thyme **3**

Essentials

Salt Cay has its own informative website (**www.saltcay.org**), which has a business directory (with listings of accommodations, restaurants, grocery stores, watersports operators, golf-cart rentals, and the like), a map of the island, history, and much more.

For information on getting to Salt Cay, as well as information about getting around the island, see "Salt Cay: Getting There & Getting Around," in chapter 6.

Exploring the Island

The island has two districts, North and South. Interestingly, some islanders rarely leave the South District and others would never deign to step outside the North District. Something about the South being the traditional, more conservative side of the island and the North the go-go business side. In any case, if you want to see all of the island—and you do—you will probably want a bike or a golf cart. Contact **Salt Cay Riders Golf Cart Rentals (© 649/ 244-1407;** two-seater golf carts $65–$75/day, $350/week; credit cards accepted).

Aside from the salinas, much interesting architecture remains from the salt-raking days of the early 19th century. The 200-year-old **Government House** has been acquired by the Turks & Caicos National Trust, which plans to restore this historic property, once the seat of government for the island. For more information, go to **http://saltcaypreservation.org**.

 Salt Cay Salt Works: Selling Salt in a Bottle

The salt industry that was the engine of the island's economy for 3 centuries officially ended more than 50 years ago, leaving the great salinas abandoned and a natural resource untapped. But now Salt Cay salt is back in business with **Salt Cay Salt Works** (www.saltcaysaltworks.com), a burgeoning cottage industry that was the brainchild of Haidee Williams. Haidee recognized the huge potential in bottling a local treasure. It's been a boon: The business is employing islanders, ingeniously recycling bottles (Brugal rum bottles from the D.R. were in plentiful supply), and providing locally made goods to the booming TCI marketplace. The Salt Cay Salt Works lineup includes premium Fleur de Sel salt, flavored culinary salts, and soaps, salts scrubs, and bath salts in pretty packages. Now you can buy Salt Cay Salt Works in stores in Grand Turk and Provo (including Maison Creole, in the airport). Contact Haidee at haidee127@gmail.com for an order form.

SALT CAY watersports operators: MASTER LIST

- **Crystal Seas Adventures/Aqua Tours** (www.crystalseas adventures.com; ☎ **649/243-9843**): The new kid on the block, helmed by Salt Cay resident, divemaster, and historian Tim Dunn, offers scuba diving/snorkeling excursions, whale-watching trips, and adventure tours on a 27-foot catamaran Pro-Cat. It specializes in small, customized outings, carrying a maximum of 6 people on scuba trips and a maximum of 10 people on non-scuba trips. The *Crystal Seas Adventure* is also available for private charters and can travel between Salt Cay and Grand Turk (weather permitting) in 15 minutes.

- **Salt Cay Adventure Tours** (www.saltcaytours.com; ☎ **649/946-6909**) is an all-purpose watersports activities operator. Led by local historian and businesswoman Candy Herwin, Salt Cay Adventure Tours can arrange scuba-diving trips (for a fully equipped PADI dive shop, see **Salt Cay Divers,** below); guide you on snorkeling, whale-watching, or snorkeling adventures; rent out bikes and kayaks; and organize island-history and art tours.

- **Salt Cay Divers** (www.saltcaydivers.tc; ☎ **649/241-1009**): A fully equipped PADI dive shop with instruction at every level, Salt Cay Divers also offers premier whale-watching excursions, sunset cruises, and snorkeling trips to nearby uninhabited islands. Its staff is well-versed in personalized service. Carolina skiffs are able to get up close to prime reefs and dive sites, and a 9.8m (32-ft.) V-hull is used for longer, smoother rides to other islands and cays. Salt Cay Divers offers a range of dive/stay packages. It also has one of the island's few stores: **Splash** boutique sells sunscreen, diving supplies, sundresses, tunics, swimwear, and cool jewelry.

The White House ★ HISTORIC HOME   The White House was built by Daniel Harriott in 1825 of Bermuda limestone. The roof alone weighs 80 tons. On the first floor is a salt storage warehouse, which leads to a boathouse where salt was transported from lighters (smaller boats) to larger vessels out in deep water. The interior is a treasure trove of artifacts from the early salt-raking days, and little has been disturbed. In one room are a wooden cradle and wooden crib, both from 1720. A ship's medicine chest—still containing bottles of poison and potash—shares a great room with bookcases filled with mid-19th-century tomes. All bedrooms are on the north side of the building to catch the breezes. The White House is said to be haunted, and there are islanders who won't pass it after dark. The White House is still owned by descendants of the Harriott family, and it is not open for commercial tours, but it can be toured by appointment.

Victoria St., Salt Cay. Tours by appointment only. Contact Crystal Seas Adventures at 𝄞 **649/243-9843** for information.

Scuba Diving ★★

The Northwest Wall, Kelly's Folly, and Turtle Garden offer wall diving at its finest—and each of these dive sites is just 5 to 10 minutes from the Salt Cay dock. Huge gorgonians, soft coral, and sponges form a backdrop for a family of spotted eagle rays, turtles, pelagics, and dolphins. Night dives let you see sleeping turtles, slipper lobsters, huge crabs, nurse sharks, and a seasonal array of other nocturnal critters.

The wreck of the **HMS *Endymion*** ★, which went down in a storm in 1790, lies off Salt Cay and near Great Sand Cay (see below). Diver and local legend Bryan Sheedy discovered the wreck 2 centuries later. Today, while the reef has reclaimed the hull and all else that was biodegradable, divers can still get a close-up look at its 18 coral- and sponge-encrusted cannons and nine huge anchors lying about. Resting in just 12m (40 ft.) of water, it's one of the region's most popular snorkel and dive sites.

All dive sites are on the island's western (leeward) side, so even if the sea is rough, you can go out diving. All boats leave from Deane's Dock (next to the Coral Reef Bar & Grill).

Snorkeling & Island Excursions ★★★

As good as the diving is around Salt Cay, the island may be an even better snorkeling destination, with some of the best snorkeling in the TCI, much of it right off the beaches. **North Shore Point, Point Pleasant, Lighthouse Cliffs,** and **South Creek** offer opportunities to see brilliantly hued fish, turtles, even the occasional barracuda steps from the beach. Just offshore, a 5-minute ride from the boat dock, the **Aquarium** is a topnotch snorkel spot in 7.6 to 9m (25–30 ft.) of water.

Increasingly popular are half- and full-day trips to **uninhabited offshore cays.** Fifteen minutes by boat from Salt Cay, **Cotton Cay** is a private natural reserve with stunning beaches and excellent snorkeling. It's a landscape of Turk's Head cactuses and heather, where ducks float on ponds and you can see the remnants of sugarcane fields. **Salt Cay Divers** (see "Salt Cay Watersports Operators: Master List," above) has exclusive access to Cotton Cay.

Some think the most gorgeous island in the TCI to be **Great Sand Cay,** with its sand so soft your feet sink into it. This uninhabited national park is a big bird-watching sanctuary and home to native iguanas. You can even camp out on the island (Salt Cay Divers has tents). On **Gibbs Cay,** you can snorkel just off the sugary-sand beach amid docile stingrays. Half- or full-day trips to Great Sand Cay and Gibbs Cay can be arranged through **Salt Cay Divers** and **Crystal Seas Adventure** (see "Salt Cay Watersports Operators: Master List," above).

Whale-Watching ★★★

Between January and April, **humpback whales** come here to play as they travel the 2,134m (7,000-ft.) trench of the Turks Island Passage to the Silver Banks in the Dominican Republic to mate and calf. Visitors can watch their antics from shore, boat out among them, or strap on dive or snorkeling equipment and go below. Salt Cay is one of the few places in the world you can actually get in the water and swim with these impressive creatures. Salt Cay Divers (see "Salt Cay Watersports Operators: Master List," above) does what is called "soft water encounters." As Debbie Manos of Salt Cay Divers explains it, "We gently slide into the water after ensuring that the whales are not frightened by our presence. Then the whales actually swim toward you. We ask that you not get too close, but believe me, those whales know exactly where you are—and if they wanted to hurt you, they would, but they are truly gentle creatures. We snorkel for a few minutes and watch their graceful bodies underwater. The usual encounter only lasts a

 Whale-Watching 101

The humpback whales that pass Salt Cay on their way to Silver Banks can be up to 15m long (50 ft.)—babies are born at 1.2m (4 ft.). Whales travel in their migration along the wall just offshore. According to Salt Cay Divers' Debbie Manos, a certified naturalist, everyone onboard is involved during whale-watching excursions. Each passenger takes up a position and reports sightings ("whale at 12 o'clock!"). Here's how you know that whales are close. The most obvious clue is whales breaching—leaping, often spectacularly—in the water. Another, less obvious clue is spray that resembles reverse rain. You can even tell when a whale has just submered by the whale "footprint" on the surface of the water: It looks like a big, dark oil slick. Of course, many people are fooled by "whale waves" that look an awful lot like whales but turn out to be, well, waves.

few minutes, but it's the thrill of a lifetime." Boats are mindful to maneuver some distance from the whales and cut the motor and drift.

Of course, on Salt Cay, you don't have to go to sea to spot a whale. Humpbacks pass so closely to shore that you can watch them from your villa deck. Debbie Manos recalls a particularly memorable sighting from the deck of the Coral Reef Bar & Grill. It was around twilight when a week-old baby whale, with dark, smooth skin, appeared. "All of a sudden we saw the mother come up under the baby and flip it in the air," Manos says. The mother was teaching the baby to jump, Manos says, and the lucky few who watched the exuberant show never even needed binoculars.

Beachcombing ★★★

Here on Salt Cay, beachcombing is an essential activity. The prevailing currents drop off bamboo tree trunks from Africa, flip-flops, and plastic floats as well as bona fide treasures like pieces of eight and an old colonial spyglass. It's not just the sea that delivers treasures; the land around the old salt-raker homes is a trove of pottery shards and vintage Blue Willow china (especially after a rain). You'll find ballast rock from old ships on the island's leeward beaches, and shiny shells on the island's South End.

Beachcombing is not just a lark for Salt Cay's Doug Gordon; it's business. The former Hollywood press agent is the artist/owner of **Beachcombers: Unique Gifts from the Sea** (Airport Rd.; no phone; drop in when the sign says OPEN), where he crafts furnishings, artwork, and jewelry out of the flotsam and jetsam he finds on the beach. Hurricane lamps are fashioned out of seashells, furniture from driftwood. His collages employ everything from dominos and donkey teeth to beach glass and colored plastic. "To be representative of a place, I have to use everything I find," Gordon says. His Salt Cay finds have included Russian sonic buoys and bottles filled with Haitian voodoo items. Gordon and his wife, Angela, kayak to the island's windward eastern side for their best finds. But Gordon knows you don't have to go far to pick up treasures on Salt Cay—some of his handsomest stones have been found right by the Coral Reef Bar & Grill.

Where to Eat

Salt Cay has a handful of limited grocery/convenience stores, among them **Netty's Store** (next door to Island Thyme restaurant) and **Pat's Store** (South Town). Netty Talbot, born and bred on Salt Cay, sells fresh-baked bread out of her store. Keep in mind that most stores keep irregular hours, and none sell alcohol. You can buy beer, wine, and liquors at **Porter's Island Thyme** or the

Coral Reef Bar & Grill. Most of the rental villas and cottages offer grocery concierge service—and you can arrive to a fully stocked fridge and pantry. Note that reservations are required for all meals at the restaurants below.

Coral Reef Bar & Grill ★ ISLAND/CONTINENTAL This, the only ocean-side cafe on island, is a live wire, with zesty margaritas and impromptu salsa dancing most any night. It's a great place to sit and watch for whales on the horizon. The Wednesday night Conch Festival serves up conch fritters, conch chowder, cracked conch, even Conch Candy: tenderized conch baked in a sugary dough. Don't miss the Sunday Barbecue Night, when Debbie and company prepare first-rate barbecued ribs, homemade slaw, and peas 'n' rice. Debbie's homemade peanut butter and chocolate pie is a smooth and satisfying finish to a hearty meal.

Victoria St., Salt Cay. © **649/241-1009.** Reservations required for all meals. $20–$25 per person dinner. Beer, wine, and liquors extra. MC, V. Daily 7am–closing.

Pat's Place ★ ISLAND Pat Simmons is a retired schoolteacher who taught for 28 years in the Salt Cay school system. Miss Pat runs this modest eatery out of her home. Enter through a wooden gate through a garden filled with tropical plants and flowers. You'll dine on the breeze-filled screened porch with tin ceiling painted green and windows with wooden shutters, open to warm salt air, waving palms, and the sounds of the neighborhood. Call ahead to say you're coming, give Pat your order, and when you arrive, you'll be treated to delicious island food served family style. Start with a simple salad. Entrees include cracked conch, fish fingers (grouper), steamed fish (with Pat's own tomato sauce), barbecued chicken, or curry conch. Sides might be stewpeas and rice, okra and rice, vegetable rice, or fried plantains. Pat's homemade pepper jelly is addictive. Ask for directions or have Pat arrange taxi service.

Historic South District. © **649/946-6919.** Reservations required for all meals. $25 per person dinner ($16 lunch). Beer and wine extra. Cash only. Mon–Sat 6:30am–9:30pm.

Porter's Island Thyme ★★ CARIBBEAN/INTERNATIONAL If this is the nerve center of Salt Cay, then its ebullient owner, Porter Williams, is its commander. Island Thyme is more than just a place to eat—it's the local bank, the Wi-Fi center, and party central. Where else can you sip a cool Cuba Libre while cheering on a hermit crab race? Where else can you dine on filet mignon, sip a vintage Bordeaux, and then walk home in your bare feet under a canopy of stars? Islanders, expats, rich, poor: They all come to Porter's for good cheer and sustenance. When the place is filled with chatter and Porter is behind the bar, Island Thyme feels like the soulful center of the world. Open for breakfast, lunch, and dinner, the restaurant has a lively bar scene—ask about the Wolf shooter, but sign everything you own over to a trusted family member before imbibing. At night, sample such delicacies as Filipino egg rolls, coconut shrimp, and Asian-inspired "jumping steak"—tender pieces of marinated and sautéed steak. Porter has a cellar of more than 100 wines, and a demonstration kitchen is in the works. You can buy the colorful Haitian art on the walls (and crawling up the ceiling), and half of the money raised on Bingo Night goes to different local charities. A roof deck has comfortable seating (plump pillows) for watching the sunset. Not to be outdone, a Congo African Gray Parrot named Charlie lives out on the porch, and if you sing a stanza of "Old MacDonald Had a Chicken," he'll do a little jig and maybe sing a few bars.

Salt Cay. www.islandthyme.tc. © **649/946-6977** or 649/242-0325. Reservations required for all meals. Main courses $19–$30 (seafood paella for 2 or 3 $60). MC, V. Daily 7–9am, noon–2pm, and 6:30–9pm. Closed 1 day a week in the off season and 2 months a year (generally 2 weeks in May and Sept–Oct).

Where to Stay

The choice of lodging in Salt Cay is limited to villas, cottages, and small guesthouses; the island has no hotel or resort lodging. The whimsical and wonderful **Windmills Plantation** did not survive the hurricanes of 2008. The resort had been in operation since 1980, its construction the stuff of a fascinating book, *The Carnival Never Got Started,* by the man who built it, Guy Lovelace. What remains lies in ruins—and is being discreetly salvaged—on North Beach, one of the best beaches on the island and a top snorkeling spot.

At press time the development of a major luxury resort on Salt Cay was on hold pending the outcome of government corruption inquiries. The development company (DevCo) planned an extensive eco-resort and 18-hole championship golf course.

Castaway, Salt Cay ★ If you're looking for privacy, utter serenity, and proximity to a gorgeous, secluded beach, this is the spot for you. A mile from Balfour Town and Island Thyme restaurant, these four comfortable one-bedroom suites (in two separate cottages) are mere feet away from the powdery sands of North Beach. You can walk the length of the beach (4km/2½ miles) and never see another footprint in the sand. Across the sea are the glittering lights of the Grand Turk Cruise Center, and in the winter you can watch whales from your porch. Each suite comes with a handsome king-size bed and a fully equipped kitchen. You'll have the use of a golf cart to travel the rough, unpaved road between Balfour Town and Castaway—slow down for donkeys and cows—and at night it's a magical trip, just you and a tapestry of stars.

A villa STAY IN SALT CAY

The island has a number of **villas and cottages** to rent, most with full self-catering capabilities and maid service. The elegant waterfront **Villas of Salt Cay** (Victoria St.; www.thevillasofsaltcay.com; ✆ **649/241-1009** or 772/713-9502; $395–$475/night high season; $150–$240/night off season; ask about rates for entire complex) has three lodging options: the Villa Frangipani, a two-story main house that accommodates six people; the Villa Olivewood, an efficiency apartment that accommodates four; and the Cabanas of the Villas, three connected one-room efficiencies. All three villas are set in a sprawling walled compound ringing a freshwater pool, and all three open onto a deck that overlooks the ocean. The two-unit **Vistas of Salt Cay** (www.saltcay.net; $150–$225 high season; $125–$200 off season) enjoys the same oceanfront setting as the Villas but is more modest in decor and space (and rates). Both units have one bedroom, and the beach out front is a nice spot to snorkel.

Sink into historic Salt Cay in the beautifully restored **Brown House** (also known as Sunnyside; www.saltcaywaterfront.com; ✆ **649/244-1407**; $850/night; $5,250/week; ask about specials and off-season rates). The oldest house on island was built in 1820 and has an old "battery," a kitchen set off from the house (now outfitted to the nines and fit for a professional chef),a breeze-filled wraparound porch, and three en-suite bedrooms. The mammoth first floor is the original salt storage room and was crafted of ship timbers and wooden pegs. Another stunning historic restoration, the British-Colonial **Half Way House** (www.halfwayhousesaltcay.com; ✆ **561/835-9237**; $4,800/week high season; $3,900/week off season) has impeccable antique furnishings, three bedrooms, and an elegant tiled deck overlooking the sea. Watch the whales from your deck at **Charming House Villa** (www.charminghousevilla.com; ✆ **772/713-9502**; $750/week high season; $575/week off season). This traditional two-story Bermudan Cape was once home to beloved Salt Cay Belonger Felix Lightbourne. It accommodates six people and has three bedrooms and a fully equipped kitchen.

For an updated directory of Salt Cay villas, go to **www.salt cay.org**.

5

THE TURKS ISLANDS | Salt Cay

North Beach, Salt Cay, Turks and Caicos, B.W.I. www.castawaysonsaltcay.com. ✆/fax **649/946-6977.** 4 units. Suites $175–$265/nightly; $1,225–$1,855/weekly. Extra person $50 per night. Meal plans available at Island Thyme restaurant. MC, V. *In room:* Ceiling fan, kitchen.

Pirate's Hideaway   Proprietor and local historian Candy Herwin has created a lush hideaway with this sweet little guesthouse. In addition to three one-bedroom suites, you can stay in Blackbeard's Quarters, a vintage salt-raker cottage with four bedrooms (one en suite), a big covered patio for dining, and a fully equipped kitchen. Each spacious suite is uniquely furnished; the Butterfly Suite has a big, sunny, airy kitchen that feels like home. Pirate's Hideaway faces the beach and Periwinkle Park (a miniature nature reserve) and has a lovely freshwater pool with tropical landscaping and a deck for barbecuing. You can sit out on the balcony of the second-floor Sunset Suite and watch whales breaching.

Victoria St., Salt Cay, Turks and Caicos, B.W.I. www.pirateshideaway.com. ℂ/fax **649/946-6909.** 4 units. Suite $75–$225; Blackbeard's Quarters $400–$450. Dive packages available. Golf-cart rentals available. MC, V. **Amenities:** Gym, freshwater pool. *In room:* A/C, ceiling fan, TV, kitchen or kitchentte.

Tradewinds Guest Suites   Tradewinds offers five one-bedroom self-catering suites steps away from the sea beneath the shade of casuarina trees. Each suite has a full kitchen or kitchenette, one bedroom, living room with sofa bed, private bathroom, and a screened porch. You can ask the staff to stock food for your arrival, or choose an all-inclusive meal plan at Coral Reef Bar & Grill (see above) and dive package. Taxes are included in the rates.

Victoria St., Salt Cay, Turks and Caicos, B.W.I. www.tradewinds.tc ℂ **649/ 241-1009.** Fax 649/946-6940. 5 units. Winter $190 single or double; off season $161 single or double. Each additional person up to 4 people $20 per night. Children 11 and under free in parent's room. Weekly rates available. Ask about meal and dive packages. MC, V. **Amenities:** Bikes; barbecue grills; hammocks; Wi-Fi (free, at the Coral Reef Bar & Grill). *In room:* A/C on request, ceiling fan, kitchen.

PLANNING YOUR TRIP TO THE TURKS & CAICOS ISLANDS

This chapter tackles the basics of a trip to the TCI, including everything from finding airfares to deciding whether to rent a car. But first, let's start with some background information about this island destination.

GETTING TO KNOW THE TURKS & CAICOS

For years, this nation of low-lying coral islands southeast of the Bahamas was little more than a slumbering backwater, home to a close-knit society of islanders called "Belongers," many of them descendants of African slaves brought to the islands by British Loyalists in the late 18th century to work the cotton plantations. When cotton went bust as an island crop, the Brits moved on, leaving the slaves behind. So for some 250 years, these freed slaves had the islands pretty much to themselves (save for a sampling of beach bums, sailors, divers, and smugglers). This swathe of real estate with which they were left included an 805km (500-mile) coral reef system—the world's third-largest—and some of the most breathtaking beaches on the planet.

But the Turks and Caicos Islands are undiscovered no more: Overnight, it seems, this sun-kissed archipelago has become synonymous with tropical island luxury. The island chain—especially Providenciales (nicknamed Provo)—has quickly become one of the fastest-growing resort destinations in the Caribbean. Lining the 19km (12 miles) of Provo's Grace Bay Beach is an impressive roster of world-class accommodations that few other rookie Caribbean destinations can claim. It's mind-boggling, really: Follow this long, sinuous stretch of sand and you'll pass such heavyweights as Club Med, Point Grace, the Somerset, the Regent Palms, the Gansevoort, and Beaches. And just offshore is celebrity magnet Parrot Cay, the determinedly low-tech exclusivity of the Meridian Club, and the Turks & Caicos Sporting Club (a Greenbrier affiliate) on Ambergris Cay, in South Caicos.

In fact, things were going swimmingly, with resorts ratcheting up the luxe factor, until the islands were hit with a triple whammy: the devastating hurricane of 2008, the global recession, and the country's own little constitutional crisis (see "A Fine Mess," below). In 2009, the boom came to a thudding halt. Projects stalled or went into receivership. Nikki Beach, the glitzy nightclub brand, shut down its resort in Leeward in 2009. Construction on the much-touted Ritz-Carlton project on West Caicos came to a stop, and plans to zap sweet little Salt Cay into a luxury golf resort were put on ice. Perhaps the biggest thud heard 'round the islands was the demise of the much-ballyhooed resort on Dellis Cay, one of the Caicos Cays, where a handful of world-renowned "starchitects" was tapped to design a Mandarin Oriental hotel, villas, and home-sites starting at around $2 million.

 A Fine Mess

The first 10 years of the 21st century were tempestuous ones for the TCI: The islands were buffeted by hurricanes, a global recession, and a messy government scandal. In 2009, the U.K. took the unprecedented steps of stripping this British colony of its powers of self-governance, suspending its constitution, and installing a British governor (temporarily, it's hoped)—measures taken after an official Commission of Inquiry found a "culture of corruption" at the highest levels of government. Court documents told of government ministers and the relatives of high-ranking officers transacting shady development deals for boatloads of money—such as the building of an environmentally suspect man-made island in Leeward harbor—and granting highly prized "Belonger-ship" (citizenship status) to folks of dubious belongering. But the most riveting testimony revolved around the extravagant lifestyle of former premier Michael Misick, including his rocky and short-lived marriage to Hollywood star LisaRaye McCoy. At press time, Mr. Misick and his cohorts were awaiting sentencing and facing the very real possibility of serving time in jail for their misdeeds.

Even through boom and bust, the Turks and Caicos Islands have retained their epic good looks and "what, me worry?" disposition. And at press time there were stirrings of life in the unfinished resorts that hover over pricey beachfronts. The West Caicos project is reportedly back on, and Dellis Cay has supposedly acquired a new owner. With a larger airport welcoming a record number of visitors to the islands and the Grand Turk Cruise Center deemed an unqualified success, the TCI is bouncing back.

Why the TCI?

Why was Turks & Caicos ripe for all this tourism development in the first place? For North Americans, the TCI has a number of enticing attributes: English is the official language, the U.S. dollar is the local currency, and the islands have become easily accessible by plane. Nonstop flights out of New York City (3 hr.), Boston (3½ hr.), Charlotte (2 hr.), and Miami (1½ hr.) mean you can jump on a plane in the morning and be lazing about on a tropical beach by early afternoon.

The country's beaches, water, and coral reef system are exquisitely beautiful and relatively unspoiled. The seas have an intense cerulean hue that puts Technicolor to shame. The climate is best described as "eternal summer": ideal year-round. Trade winds blow in from the east, a gentle tickle of relief from the buttery sun.

And until the economy went, well, south, the islands also enjoyed zero unemployment—although much of its work force is now drawn from places like Haiti, Jamaica, and even the Philippines (the native TCI population is relatively small). And even though crime has risen with the building boom, you simply do not see the kind of impoverishment that plagues other Caribbean countries.

The island citizens—"the Belongers"—enjoy one of the best primary and secondary educational systems in the region. The Belongers share a warm, wry familiarity, and it's easy to see why many have embraced the possibility that they are all connected by blood—descendants either of slaves imported to the islands centuries ago, or of the 193 African slaves freed on these isolated islands when the slave ship *Trouvadore,* carrying them to lives of bondage in Cuba, wrecked on the East Caicos reef in 1841. Research is underway by a Turks & Caicos National Museum expedition team to discern whether a shipwreck found off East Caicos in 2004 is the *Trouvadore*—and if so, whether its inhabitants were indeed the progenitors of the modern-day Belongers. For the latest information, go to www.tcmuseum.org/projects/slave-ship-trouvadore.

A LITTLE history

The earliest inhabitants of these islands were Lucayan Indians, who settled here some 800 years before Columbus arrived in the New World. Some historians believe that Grand Turk was the site of Columbus's first landfall—and experts have established that the explorer was indeed greeted on his arrival by Lucayan Indians—but little hard evidence exists to support this theory either way. The Lucayans' idyllic existence came to an end when Spanish explorers arrived, enslaving the natives and exposing them to disease. In a generation, the Lucayan population was wiped out. Habitation was spotty after that, with the islands passing through Spanish, French, and British control and industries coming and going—from salt-raking, which drew Bermudans in the late 17th century, to cotton, which brought British Loyalists fleeing the States after the American Revolution. An anemic cotton industry was eventually done in by storms and pests, and by the early 19th century, the main inhabitants left on the islands were the slaves that had been brought in to work the plantations. But it was raking and making salt that was the islands' main industry; at one point Salt Cay was the premier provider of salt in the world. The salt industry—back-breaking, labor-intensive work made more so by the tropical heat—was nationalized in 1951 but was not officially over until the 1960s, around the same time that a small airstrip was built on Provo and a nascent tourism industry began to stir. In 1984, the development of Club Med led to the construction of a larger airport, and commercial tourism started to take root in the TCI.

Those concerned that the TCI is in danger of being ruinously developed will take comfort in knowing that of its 40 islands, only 10 are inhabited. The most populous beach, Provo's Grace Bay, still has long, dreamy stretches where you're the only soul on the soft sand. Even throughout the giddy boom times, the general focus has been on sustainable development and low-impact, high-end properties (boutique resorts with ecologically sensitive outlooks). And the combination of financial recession and constitutional crisis may have been something of a blessing in disguise—a necessary stopgap for a runaway train. With things moving at a slightly slower pace, perhaps the business side will be more in tune with the natural rhythms of this island nation—essential for the survival of both.

TURKS & CAICOS at a glance

Location: The Turks and Caicos archipelago is located in the British West Indies, 48km (30 miles) south of the Bahamas, 161km (100 miles) northeast of the Dominican Republic, and 925km (575 miles) southeast of Miami. Even though it's considered to be part of the Caribbean region, the TCI is not officially in the Caribbean because it's not in the Caribbean Sea—like the Bahamas, it's in the Atlantic Ocean.

Population: The country's population is approximately 30,000 people, of which approximately 12,000 to 15,000 are native "Belongers," TCI citizens who are primarily the descendants of African slaves. A large group of Haitian expats live and work in the TCI (many of them so long that they have been granted Belonger status). Other sizeable expat populations include Jamaicans, Dominican Republicans, Canadians, Brits, and Americans.

Size: The two island groups—the Turks islands and the Caicos islands—together comprise 500 sq. km (193 sq. miles) and are separated by the 35km (22-mile) **Columbus Passage,** a deep sea channel that delivered Christopher Columbus into the New World in 1492.

Economy: Tourism, fishing, and the offshore finance industry are the big three. Regarding the latter, the islands are a "zero tax" jurisdiction and charge no taxes on income, capital gains, corporate profits, inheritance, or estates. There are no controls on transferring funds or assets in or out of the country.

Government: The TCI is a British Crown Colony. A queen-appointed governor holds executive power and presides over an Executive Council. A 1987 constitution established a representative democracy, and today the local government is elected by the citizens and includes a premier (the country's first), a deputy premier, other ministers, and a legislative council empowered to enact local statutes. The TCI seat of government is Cockburn Town in Grand Turk. *Note:* At press time, corruption concerns have led the British government to suspend the constitution and assume governance of the island. The plan is to return self-rule to the island once governmental safeguards have been put into place.

Last time the queen visited: 1966. Elizabeth II stopped in at South Caicos for the day, sailing in on the royal yacht *Britannia.*

THE ISLANDS IN BRIEF

Most of the TCI is low-lying, with sandy soil and a low scrub cover, but each island has its own unique look and feel. North Caicos, the so-called garden island, is a sprawling rural landscape rimmed by blue-green seas. Middle Caicos is a knockout, with emerald cliffs overlooking sharp-toothed iron-shore coves, pillowy beaches fringed by casuarina trees, and plantation ruins (and the occasional cotton or sisal plant). Grand Turk, Salt Cay, and South Caicos are culturally laid-back and contain abandoned salinas and other colonial architecture, while much in Provo (Providenciales) is as bright and shiny as a new penny. All have stupendous soft-sand beaches lapped by tranquil azure seas.

In an interesting twist, the boom that hit Provo has drawn people to tourism-industry jobs away from their homes—and traditional livelihoods—on the other islands. In Middle Caicos in particular, you'll see tabby homes of limestone and shells abandoned to the underbrush, and once-thriving communities reduced to ghost towns. To ensure that the traditional cultures and way of life on the islands aren't lost forever, the **Turks & Caicos National Trust** has made it its mission to "safeguard the natural, historical and cultural heritage of the Turks and Caicos Islands." To find out more about the National Trust's latest projects, go to the website **http://tcinationaltrust.org**.

The Caicos Islands

PROVIDENCIALES The 98-sq.-km (38-sq.-mile) island of **Providenciales (Provo)** and its splendid 19km (12-mile) Grace Bay Beach were a tourist mecca waiting to happen. In the 1980s, Club Med and Le Deck (now Sibonné) were the only resorts on Grace Bay, until the government opened the door to boutique resort development. Now Provo's tourist infrastructure far surpasses anything on Grand Turk, the TCI seat of government. This is where the action is, literally, as Provo is home to the bulk of the country's lodging, dining, tours, activities, and entertainment. Still, don't expect a bustling metropolis: Provo is still a pretty laid-back place to be, and that's a big part of its charm. One of the larger islands of the Turks and Caicos, Provo is largely flat and arid, with miles of scrubland. Today, Provo is the entry point and main destination for most visitors to the TCI.

CAICOS CAYS Also called the Leeward Cays, these gorgeous little islands were once the lair of pirates. Many are still uninhabited except by day-trippers beachcombing and snorkeling the shallows, while others are private islands with secluded resorts. Little

Water Cay is a National Trust nature reserve and home to the endangered rock iguana.

NORTH CAICOS   Former TCI Premier Michael Misick once called North, his birthplace, "a tiger awakening." The projected site of the second big TCI boom remains a sleepy rural landscape, however. Roads are much improved, and a deepwater harbor built to accommodate freight-bearing ships (and a ferry between North and Provo) has been completed. But the beaches remain unspoiled, and lodgings and restaurants few and far between. Locals say this sparsely populated, 106-sq.-km (41-sq.-mile) island is a snapshot of Provo before the boom.

MIDDLE CAICOS   The largest island in the Turks and Caicos (125 sq. km/48 sq. miles), Middle Caicos has a correspondingly small full-time population (300 people). It's a landscape of contrasts. Soft green slopes overlook beautiful Mudjin Harbor. Along the rise is Crossing Place Trail, a narrow 18th-century path so named because it leads to a place where people once crossed a sandbar at low tide to reach North Caicos. A massive aboveground limestone cave system used by Lucayan Indians some 600 years ago makes for great exploring. At Bambarra Beach sapphire shallows stretch long into the horizon. Middle has little of Provo's tourism infrastructure; it attracts visitors who don't mind roughing it a bit amid a gorgeous seaside landscape and outdoorsmen drawn to pristine bonefishing flats. Key to delivering more traffic to the island is a causeway that links Middle to North Caicos. It was (reportedly) built on the cheap and has been roughed up by hurricanes, so it's a bumpy, bumpy ride—but a major upgrade is said to be in the works.

SOUTH CAICOS   Hard hit by Hurricane Ike in 2008, this still-sleepy fishing community of some 1,200 people and 21 sq. km (8 sq. miles) is hearing faint rumblings of tourist development. The "Big South" remains rough and ready, however, and because tourist infrastructure is still in its infancy, this guide addresses the region only peripherally. But clearly, with its excellent diving and bonefishing opportunities and upgraded airport, South Caicos is an up-and-coming spot.

EAST CAICOS   This unspoiled, uninhabited 47-sq.-km (18-sq.-mile) island was once the home of large sisal and cotton plantations and the East Caicos Cattle Company. Now it's largely swampland and savanna and a few wild donkeys—but it's a great place to reach by boat and explore.

WEST CAICOS   This lovely 29-sq.-km (11-sq.-mile) island (with a 202-hectare/500-acre nature preserve) is the site of some of the islands' best scuba diving and the wreck of the *Molasses Reef,* a 16th-century galleon that's one of the oldest European shipwrecks in the Americas. A long-awaited five-star Ritz-Carlton resort project was said to be back on track at press time.

The Turks Islands

GRAND TURK   People who only visit Provo miss out on experiencing the country's rich heritage. Enchanting Grand Turk, just 11×3km (7×2 miles), has colorful 19th-century Bermudan architecture, abandoned salinas where the business of salt-raking was conducted from the late 17th century until the 1960s, a 19th-century lighthouse, and a first-rate museum housed in the 180-year-old Guinep House. The small-town atmosphere of Cockburn Town belies the fact that this Grand Turk village is the capital of the TCI. The diving here along the continental shelf wall is stupendous, traditionally the big draw for most visitors. That certainly was the case until 2006, when Carnival Cruise Lines opened a theme-park-style cruise terminal at the southwest end of the island to welcome the arrival of 2,000-passenger ships. Now ships are in port 4 to 7 days a week—and it's been a boon for local tour operators, taxi drivers, and entrepreneurs. Still, Grand Turk remains relatively undeveloped, with just a scattering of inns and restaurants. Among the uninhabited cays in the Grand Turk Cays Land and Sea National Park is Gibbs Cay, where you can swim in clear, shallow water among stingrays.

SALT CAY   Salt Cay (pop. 60) is the kind of place where you can paste salvaged flip-flops onto your neighbor's boat while he's away, and everyone (including your neighbor) thinks it's a hoot. It's the kind of place where a hermit crab race is the talk of the town. It's also the kind of place where people come from around the world to partake in watersports activities (snorkeling, diving, whale-watching), swim in the luminescent green sea, and comb the secluded beaches for flotsam and jetsam. Salt Cay is admittedly small (6.5 sq. km/2½ sq. miles) and missing many of the basic accouterments of 21st-century civilization (one ATM, just a handful of cars), but it is also the site of significant colonial-era buildings and at press time was under consideration for World Heritage Site status.

VISITOR INFORMATION

The **Turks & Caicos Tourist Board** (www.turksandcaicos tourism.com) has offices in Stubbs Diamond Plaza, Providenciales (© 649/946-4970), and Front Street, Cockburn Town, Grand Turk (© 649/946-2321). The New York City office is now overseen by Pamela Ewing (© **800/241-0824** or 646/375-8830). In Canada, the tourist board has an office at 175 Bloor St. East, Ste. 307, South Tower, Toronto, ON (© **866/413-8875** or 416/642-9771).

INTERNET RESOURCES Whenever possible throughout this book, we've included Web addresses along with phone numbers and addresses for attractions, outfitters, and other companies. We've also given the Web address of each hotel and resort; it's a good idea to take a look at the website to get a better idea of a property before you make a reservation. In addition, most hotels have special package deals only offered on their websites.

The following recommended Turks & Caicos–specific websites can be of enormous help in planning your trip:

o **www.turksandcaicos.tc**: The TCI Mall, sponsored by LIME, the telephone and Internet provider in the TCI, is an exhaustive source of information. It's best in providing local community information (the local newspapers are linked here) and offers a thorough rundown of each island (including the less-traveled islands).

o **http://turksandcaicoshta.com**: The official site of the Turks & Caicos Hotel and Tourism Association.

o **http://tcmuseum.org**: The **Turks & Caicos National Museum** (p. 92) is a delight. This website is an informative reflection of the museum's collection, the islands' history and culture, and the ongoing research projects affiliated with the museum.

o **www.nationaltrust.tc**: The website of the Turks & Caicos National Trust, a nonprofit, nongovernmental organization dedicated to the preservation of the cultural, historical, and natural heritage of the Turks and Caicos Islands.

o **www.timespub.tc**: The website of the *Times of the Islands,* a terrific quarterly magazine that has meaty features on TCI flora and fauna, history, culture, food, and business.

WHEN TO GO
Weather

Beyond the idyllic seas and beaches, the weather here is a big draw. The average temperature on the Turks and Caicos Islands ranges between 85° and 90°F (29°–32°C) from June to October, sometimes reaching the mid-90s (35°C), especially in the late summer months. From November to May the average temperature is 80° to 84°F (27°–29°C).

Water temperature in the summer is 82° to 84°F (28°–29°C) and in winter about 74° to 78°F (23°–26°C). A constant easterly trade wind keeps the climate very comfortable.

Grand Turk and South Caicos have an annual rainfall of 53 centimeters (21 in.), but as you travel farther west, the average rainfall can increase to as much as 102 centimeters (40 in.). In an average year the TCI has 350 days of sunshine.

Mosquitoes and no-see-'ums can be a problem year-round. However, more mosquitoes come out during the rainy season, which usually occurs in autumn.

If you come in the summer, be prepared for broiling sun in the midafternoon.

For a more precise idea of what the weather will be like at the time you're visiting, check the Weather Channel's online 10-day forecast at **www.weather.com**.

Average Temperatures & Rainfall in Turks & Caicos

	JAN	FEB	MAR	APR	MAY	JUNE	JULY	AUG	SEPT	OCT	NOV	DEC
MAX (°F)	82	82	84	86	88	90	90	91	88	88	86	86
MAX (°C)	28	28	29	30	31	32	32	33	31	31	30	30
MIN (°F)	75	70	72	73	77	79	79	82	81	77	75	72
MIN (°C)	21	21	22	23	25	26	26	28	27	25	24	22
AVE. RAIN (IN.)	2.0	1.4	1.1	1.4	2.5	1.7	1.7	2.0	3.2	3.9	4.0	2.8
AVE. RAIN (CM)	5.1	3.6	2.8	3.6	6.4	4.3	4.3	5.1	8.1	9.9	10.2	7.1

Source: Hutchinson World Weather Guide

HURRICANES   The curse of Caribbean weather, the hurricane season lasts—officially, at least—from June 1 to November 30. But there's no cause for panic: Satellite forecasts give enough warning that precautions can be taken.

Until Hurricane Ike pummeled Grand Turk and South Caicos in 2008 (in the immediate wake of a drenching by Hurricane Hanna), the Turks and Caicos had been largely spared any serious hurricane havoc since 1960, when Hurricane Donna dropped 51 centimeters (20 in.) of rain in 24 hours. Some say the mountains of Haiti and the Dominican Republic weaken hurricane-force winds before the storms reach the TCI. Still, hurricanes have wreaked havoc here in the past, including a September 1926 storm that brought 240kmph (150-mph) winds, slammed boulders on beaches, and had a storm surge that moved 1.2km (¾ mile) inland. And of course, Hurricane Ike in 2008 caused enormous destruction on Grand Turk—some 80% of the island's structures were damaged.

Always monitor weather reports if you plan to visit during hurricane season. Check the **Weather Channel** on the Web at **www.weather.com**.

The High Season & the Off Season

Like much of the Caribbean, the Turks and Caicos have become a year-round destination. The "season" runs roughly from mid-December to mid-April, which is generally the driest time of year in the Caribbean and the most miserable time of year in the northern U.S. and in Canada. Hotels charge their highest prices during the peak winter period, and you'll have to make your reservations well in advance—months in advance if you want to travel over the Christmas or New Year's holidays or in the depths of February, especially around Presidents' Day weekend. The Easter holidays/ school spring break is an increasingly popular time for families to visit.

The off season in the Turks and Caicos—roughly from mid-April to mid-November—is generally an ideal time to come to the TCI: Yes, the temperatures are somewhat higher, but the southeasterly trade winds work to temper the heat, as do the brief but more frequent rain showers. The off season is also one big sale. In most cases, hotels, inns, and condos slash 20% to 50% off their winter rates. Airfares are generally cheaper, and air/hotel packages can be quite reasonable, even for stays at the top luxury lodgings. For Europeans, who generally have longer vacation times, the summer is already a popular time to visit the TCI.

Note: Some hotels use the off season for refurbishment or bustling construction projects—which can be an annoyance if you're looking for peace and quiet. Make sure to ask what, if any, work is going on. If you decide to book anyway, ask for a room away from the noise.

Holidays

New Year's Day (Jan 1); Commonwealth Day (observed on the Mon nearest Mar 12); Good Friday (celebrated the Fri prior to Easter); Easter Monday (celebrated on the Mon after Easter); National Heroes Day (observed the last Mon in May in honor of the First Chief Minister, the late Hon. J.A.G.S. McCartney); Queen's Official Birthday (observed mid-June); Emancipation Day (celebrated the first of Aug; this holiday commemorates the freedom of the slaves, which was declared from Oddfellows Lodge in Grand Turk in 1834); National Youth Day (celebrated the last Fri of Sept); Columbus Day (celebrated on the Mon nearest Oct 10; this holiday commemorates Christopher Columbus's "landing" on TCI in 1492—although no firm evidence exists to confirm that the explorer actually made a landfall here at all); International Human Rights Day (observed on Oct 24; this holiday is similar to the U.S. July Fourth celebration); Christmas Day (Dec 25); Boxing Day

(Dec 26; on this day the annual Church Fair takes place in the Grand Turk Methodist Church).

Turks & Caicos Calendar of Events

JANUARY

Junkanoo, island-wide. These regional street festivals are held throughout the year for public holidays and local events, but the biggest Junkanoo celebrations are on Emancipation Day, Boxing Day, and the early morning of New Year's Day. Groups compete against each other for the most outrageous costumes, the best drummers, the best rhythm section, and more. Midnight to sunrise, New Year's Day morning.

FEBRUARY

Valentine's Day Cup, Bambarra Beach, Middle Caicos. Traditional Model Sailboat Regatta, with trophies and other prizes, is followed by music, dancing, food, and other festivities on the beach. The model sailboats are built in Bambarra from branches of the gum-elemi tree, constructed to scale with the actual rigging found on a full-size sloop. For more information, contact ℂ **649/941-7639** or **middlecaicos@tciway.tc**. Saturday closest to Valentine's Day.

MARCH

Paddy's Pub Crawl, Providenciales. Now in its 20th year, the crawl generally starts at the Tiki Hut and ends up at Danny Buoy's, with lots of suds along the way. Contact ℂ **649/231-1645.** March 17.

APRIL

Annual Kite-Flying Competition, Children's Park, Lower Bight Road, Providenciales. These annual competitions feature awards for best homemade kites, a beach party, an Easter egg hunt, and food and music. Call ℂ **649/946-4970** for dates.

Salt Cay Splashdown Days, Salt Cay. Three days of food, music, pageants, kite flying, dancing, and fun. Contact Porter Williams at pwiii@aol.com for dates and additional information.

MAY

Big South Regatta, South Caicos. The Big South Regatta, a tradition since 1967, features boat races, concerts, food, and entertainers. Contact ℂ **649/946-4970.** Last weekend in May.

JUNE

Fools' Regatta, Children's Park, the Bight, Providenciales. This beach party celebrating all things maritime and features native sloops in sailing races and a sand-castle competition. The regatta is held to raise funds for local causes. For more information, call the Turks & Caicos Tourist Board at ℂ **649/946-4970.** Mid-June.

SummaJam Festival & Grand Turk Heineken Game Fishing Tournament, Grand Turk. Fish tourney and island party at Governor's Beach features cash prizes, music, barbecue, volleyball, and, of course, dominoes.

For more information, call the Turks & Caicos Tourist Board at © **649/946-2321.** Late June weekend.

JULY

Caicos Classic Annual Release Tournament, Providenciales. This international billfishing tournament is based in Provo. For more information, e-mail Art at **art@caicosclassic.com** or call © **649/941-3781.** Call for dates.

AUGUST

Emancipation Day, island-wide. Celebrating the freeing of the slaves, declared from Oddfellows Lodge in Grand Turk in 1834. August 1.

Middle Caicos Day, Middle Caicos. Parades, beauty pageants, music, food, bonfires, straw-weaving competitions, and an all-day beach party at Bambarra Beach. Contact © **649/941-7639** or **middlecaicos@tciway.tc**. Last weekend in August.

SEPTEMBER

National Youth Day, island-wide. This public holiday celebrates the youth of the islands. September 29.

OCTOBER

TCI Amateur Open, Providenciales. PricewaterhouseCoopers Limited sponsors this 3-day, 36-hole championship for both men and women, now in its 17th year, at the Provo Golf & Country Club. For more information, go to **www.provogolfclub.com**. Early October.

Columbus Day, island-wide. This public holiday celebrates Columbus's "discovery" of the New World. Some historians believe that the explorer first came ashore at Grand Turk. October 9.

NOVEMBER

Museum Day, Grand Turk. The Turks & Caicos National Museum celebrates the anniversary of its opening with loads of activities, including song and dance performances by local schoolchildren. For more information, go to **www.tcmuseum.org** or call © **649/946-2160.** Saturday closest to November 21 (the day the museum opened in 1991).

Caribbean Food & Wine Festival, Providenciales. Sample fabulous fare from the TCI's top chefs in roving gourmet safaris and food and wine tastings. For details, go to www.caribbeanfoodandwinefestivaltci. First weekend in November.

Turks & Caicos Conch Festival, Providenciales. This is becoming the islands' premier event, and the conch-etition gets fiercer every year as local restaurants vie to win top honors for best conch concoctions, including conch chowder, conch curry, and conch salad. Now in its sixth year, the conch festival is a popular celebration, with music, food, conch-blowing, and a great seaside Blue Hills location. For more information, call © **649/331-6832** or go to www.conchfestival.com. Last Saturday in November.

DECEMBER

Christmas Tree-Lighting Ceremony, Providenciales. The Providenciales Kiwanis Club invites the public to the Downtown Ball Park for Christmas festivities, including a choir and a visit from Santa Claus. Mid-December.

Island Thyme Annual Salt Cay Children's Party, Salt Cay. It's pizza and Christmas pizazz at this popular and always festive restaurant. For more information, call © **649/946-6977.** December 23.

Maskanoo, Providenciales. A mix of Junkanoo and masquerade, Maskanoo showcases the best of the islands' cultural heritage with local music, island food, arts and entertainment, a fireworks display, and a street jump-up. For more information, call the Turks & Caicos Tourist Board (© **649/946-4970**). December 23.

Old Year's Night, island-wide. Services at churches all over the country ring out the old and ring in the new. December 31.

ENTRY REQUIREMENTS
Passports

U.S. and Canadian citizens must have a passport or a combination of a birth certificate and photo ID, plus a return or ongoing ticket, to enter the country. Citizens of the United Kingdom, Commonwealth countries of the Caribbean, the Republic of Ireland, and E.U. countries must also have a current passport.

All travelers coming from the Caribbean, including Americans, are now required to have a passport to enter or reenter the United States. Those returning to Canada are also required to show passports. These requirements apply to cruise-ship passengers as well. Driver's licenses are not acceptable as a sole form of ID.

Customs

Generally, you're permitted to bring in items intended for your personal use, including tobacco, cameras, film, and a limited supply of liquor—usually 40 ounces.

Just before you leave home, check with the Turks and Caicos Customs or Foreign Affairs department for the latest guidelines—including information on items that are not allowed to be brought into your home country—since the rules are subject to change and often contain some surprising oddities.

Upon arrival in the Turks and Caicos, you may bring in 1 quart of liquor, 200 cigarettes, 50 cigars, or 8 ounces of tobacco duty-free. There are no restrictions on cameras, film, sports equipment, or personal items, provided they aren't for resale. Absolutely no spear guns or Hawaiian slings are allowed, and the importation of firearms without a permit is also prohibited. Illegal imported drugs bring heavy fines and lengthy terms of imprisonment.

You should collect receipts for all purchases made abroad. You must also declare on your Customs form the nature and value of all gifts received during your stay abroad. If you're traveling with expensive cameras or jewelry, it's prudent to carry proof that you purchased these items in the U.S. If you purchased these types of items during an earlier trip abroad, you should carry proof that you have previously paid Customs duty on the items.

Sometimes merchants suggest a false receipt to undervalue your purchase. **Beware:** You could be involved in a sting operation—the merchant might be an informer to U.S. Customs.

If you use any medication that contains controlled substances or requires injection, carry an original prescription or note from your doctor.

For specifics on what you can bring back, download the invaluable free pamphlet *Know Before You Go* online at www.cbp.gov. (Click on "Travel," then go to "Travel Smart" and click on "Know Before You Go.") Alternatively, request the pamphlet from the **U.S. Customs and Border Protection (CBP),** 1300 Pennsylvania Ave. NW, Washington, DC 20229 (© **877/287-8667**).

U.K. citizens should contact **HM Customs & Excise** at © **0845/010-9000** (© 020/8929-0152 from outside the U.K.), or consult its website at www.hmce.gov.uk.

For a clear summary of **Canadian** Customs rules, request the booklet *I Declare* from the **Canada Border Services Agency** (© **800/461-9999** in Canada, or 204/983-3500; www.cbsa-asfc.gc.ca).

Citizens of **Australia** should request a helpful brochure available from Australian consulates or Customs offices called *Know Before You Go.* For more information, call the **Australian Customs Service** at © **1300/363-263,** or log on to www.customs.gov.au.

For **New Zealand** Customs information, contact **New Zealand Customs** at © **04/473-6099** or 0800/428-786, or log on to www.customs.govt.nz.

GETTING THERE & GETTING AROUND
Getting to the Turks & Caicos

The main point of entry for international flights into the Turks and Caicos is **Providenciales International Airport** (www.provoairport.com); Grand Turk and South Caicos also have international airports. A major upgrade for the Provo airport has been good news for fliers, since a bigger airport means more planes, more competition, and more competitive rates. Muscling in on the market in

2011 are **JetBlue** (www.jetblue.com; ⓒ **800/538-2583**), which offers daily nonstop flights from New York's JFK; and **Continental Airlines** (www.continental.com; ⓒ **800/523-3273**), which offers daily flights between Newark and Provo. **American Airlines** (www.aa.com; ⓒ **800/433-7300** in the U.S. and Canada) flies regular nonstop flights from New York, Boston, and Miami. Other airlines serving the islands include **Air Canada** (ⓒ **888/247-2262** in the U.S. and Canada; www.aircanada.ca), which has direct flights from Toronto, Montreal, and Ottawa; **WestJet** (www.westjet.com; ⓒ **888/937-8538**), which flies twice weekly from Montreal and Toronto; **Bahamas Air** (http://up.bahamasair.com; ⓒ **800/222-4262**), which flies three times weekly from Nassau; **British Airways** (www.britishairways.com; ⓒ **800/247-9297** in the U.S., 0870/850-9850 in the U.K.), which flies from London via Miami; **Delta** (www.delta.com; ⓒ **800/241-4141** in the U.S. and Canada), which flies nonstop daily from Atlanta; and **US Airways** (www.usairways.com; ⓒ **800/622-1015** in the U.S. and Canada), which flies nonstop from Charlotte (daily), Boston, and Philadelphia. **Air Turks & Caicos** (www.airturksandcaicos.com; ⓒ **649/946-4181**) has regular flights between Provo and Jamaica, Haiti, the Dominican Republic, and the Bahamas.

The Provo airport has limited tourist services. A restaurant, **Gilley's Cafe** (ⓒ **649/946-4472;** open 7 days a week for breakfast and lunch), is near the **domestic arrivals and departures** area. The **international departures** lounge has a handful of duty-free shops, including **Jai's** (ⓒ **649/941-4324**), which sells fine jewelry; **Maison Creole** (ⓒ **649/946-4748**), which sells salt products from Salt Cay, hand-woven baskets from Middle Caicos, and charming handcrafted items from Haiti; and **Turquoise Duty-Free** (ⓒ **649/946-4536**), which sells liquor and Cuban and Dominican cigars. Unfortunately, the only food source is a snack bar with microwave pizza, chips, gum, and drinks. If you have a long wait ahead of you—and hungry kids in tow—consider grabbing a grouper sandwich at Gilley's before you pass through security to the

Never on a Sunday (or a Saturday)

If you can possibly swing it, avoid flying in or out of Provo on Saturday or Sunday during peak season. These are the days when weekly villa and condo rentals turn over, and the airport is overrun with travelers arriving and departing—the result being that the Customs process at arrivals can be agonizingly slow and the departure lines long and full of (understandably) cranky kids.

departures area. Or you can consider paying to relax in the **Turks and Caicos VIP Flyers Club** lounge (http://vipflyersclub.com; ⓒ **866/587-6168** or 649/946-4000), a small, 15-guest air-conditioned lounge with Wi-Fi, sandwiches, beverages, and satellite TV. It's open from 5am till the last plane leaves the ground, and it's a relative bargain at $40 per guest. It's best to reserve a space ahead.

Consider which airlines have hubs in the airport nearest you, and, of those carriers, which have the most advantageous alliances, given your most common routes. To play the frequent-flier game to your best advantage, consult Randy Petersen's **Inside Flyer** (www. insideflyer.com). Petersen and friends review all the programs in detail and post regular updates on changes in policies and trends.

Getting Around Providenciales
FROM THE AIRPORT

Most of Provo's lodgings are an easy 15- to 20-minute taxi ride from the airport. Your hotel fee most often includes complimentary van transfers; otherwise, there are plenty of **taxis** on hand to meet arriving flights. If for some reason none are around, call your hotel or the **Provo Taxi Association** (ⓒ **649/946-5481**). Cabs are metered and rates are set by the government, but not all drivers turn on their meters, so it's a good idea to negotiate the fare before you get in the car (not only for the ride from the airport, but for any cab ride in the TCI). Expect to pay around $22 to $25 (plus tip) per couple (additional person $7.50) for a taxi from the airport to the Grace Bay area. Most taxis are vans equipped to carry more than one group of passengers, so it stands to reason that the more people on board, the lower the rate per couple.

Because the island is so large and its hotels and restaurants are so far-flung, you might find a **rental car** useful on Providenciales, but be warned: Renting a car is not particularly cheap here, what with fuel prices at $5.99 a gallon and expected to rise. The airport has several rental-car agencies (see "Rental Cars," below).

Note: In general, addresses have no street numbers, more typically just designations like "Leeward Highway," "Lower Bight Road," or simply "Providenciales."

TAXIS

If you decide to forgo a rental car, you may find yourself needing a taxi every now and then (to get back to your hotel after a dinner out, for example). Taxis are expensive—just jumping from one section of Grace Bay to another can run into double figures—and they're plentiful on Provo, but there are no designated taxi stands. You can often hail a taxi on the street, or you can have your hotel or restaurant call one for you. I also highly recommend Clayton

Cox of **3 C's Taxi Service** (℡ 649/244-1546), **Lorenzo's Taxi & Tours** (℡ 649/243-8907), **Gray's Taxi & Tours** (℡ 649/242-3166), and **Boy Hall & Son Taxi** (℡ 649/244-3894 or 649/231-6308). If you find a taxi driver you like, ask for his or her card or jot down the number on the side of the van, and avail yourself of his or her services throughout your trip. (Taxi drivers are also happy to show you around the island—but be sure to negotiate the fee upfront.) A number of Provo hotels (the Grace Bay Club being one) also include complimentary shuttle service around the Grace Bay area, including trips to the Graceway grocery store.

RENTAL CARS

Three major U.S.–based car-rental agencies with a franchise in the Turks and Caicos Islands are **Budget,** with a branch at the airport and in Downtown Provo, in the Town Centre Mall (www.budget rentacar.com; ℡ 800/472-3325 in the U.S., or 649/946-4079, -5400); **Avis,** with a branch at the airport (www.avis.tc; ℡ 800/331-1212 in the U.S. and Canada, or 649/946-4705), on Grace Bay (℡ 649/941-7557), and on Leeward Highway (℡ 649/946-8570); and **Hertz** affiliate **Mystique Car Rental,** located at the Ports of Call shopping complex on Grace Bay Road and on Old Airport Road, 2 minutes from the airport (www.hertztci.com; ℡ 649/941-3910). Cars rent for $40 to $225 a day (depending on the vehicle); collision-damage insurance costs $10 to $12 a day. The government will collect a $16 tax for each rental contract, regardless of the number of days you keep the car. For booking rental cars online, the best deals are usually found at rental-car company websites, although all the major online travel agencies also offer rental-car reservations services.

If you'd like to try your luck with a local agency, call one of the following: **Grace Bay Car Rentals and Sales** (www.gracebay carrentals.com; ℡ 649/941-8500), on Grace Bay Road across from the Seven Stars resort; **Scooter Bob's,** Turtle Cove Marina (www.provo.net/scooter; ℡ 649/946-4684), which rents jeeps, vans, and SUVs; **Turks & Caicos National Car Rental** (http://airportinntci.com/rent; ℡ 649/946-4701), which has a branch at the Airport Plaza on Airport Road (2 min. from the airport); and **Rent a Buggy** (www.rentabuggy.tc; ℡ 649/946-4158) on Leeward Highway, near Central Square. Most of these agencies offer free pickup and drop-off. Rates average from $40 to $200 per day, plus the 10% government stamp duty.

In the British tradition, **cars on all the islands drive on the left.** If you're North American, you'll have to quickly master the nuances of left-side driving and navigating roundabouts. You only need a valid driver's license from your home country to rent a vehicle.

BICYCLES & SCOOTERS

Bicycling is an ideal way to get around the flat Grace Bay area. With traffic increasing, it's wise to avoid riding in the car lanes and stick to the wide sidewalks running along both sides of the road instead (although I must say that on a recent visit I found some of the sidewalks in need of a little TLC). Many resorts, including Royal West Indies, the Grace Bay Club, and the Sands at Grace Bay, offer complimentary bikes for their guests. If not, **Caicos Wheels** (Queens Landing Plaza, Grace Bay; www.caicoswheels. com; © **649/242-6592**) rents bikes (as well as scooters) in Providenciales. It will drop off and pick up bicycles at your resort; bikes cost $15 per day (deposit required).

In addition to cars, jeeps, and SUVs, **Scooter Bob's** (Turtle Cove Marina; www.provo.net/scooter; © **649/946-4684**) rents two-passenger Yamaha scooters for $49 a day ($45 a day for 5 days or more). Advance reservations are required.

On Grand Turk, you can rent scooters and bikes at **Tony's Rentals** (www.tonyscarrental.com; © **649/946-1879**).

ON FOOT

The 19km (12 miles) of Grace Bay Beach make for lovely strolls, and sidewalks line Grace Bay Road. Take the beach route when you can and soak in the views while you're strolling—the distances are shorter and it's a cooler spot to stroll.

The Other Islands: Getting There & Getting Around

Your most likely point of entry into the Turks and Caicos will be the Providenciales International Airport. If your final destination is any of the other TCI islands, you will probably be taking either a **domestic flight** on a small plane from the Provo airport or traveling **by boat** or **ferry** (generally from Walkin Marina at Heaving Down Rock, in Leeward on Provo's northeast coast, about 20 min. from the airport; to get there you'll need to take a taxi from the airport if your hotel doesn't offer airport transfers). Be aware that interisland travel and brisk efficiency are not necessarily synonymous; the weather has a lot to do with it, but so does the sleepy-lidded pace of things. Get a couple of good books and just cozy up to that velvety breeze.

Keep in mind that small airlines have **weight restrictions,** which means you may have to store any heavier luggage in the Provo airport during your trip. At press time, the maximum weight for checked luggage on a Caicos Express flight was 44 pounds.

Note: In general, addresses in the TCI have no street numbers, more typically just designations like "Leeward Highway," "Lower Bight Road," or simply "Providenciales."

CAICOS CAYS

The Caicos Cays are reachable by **boat, private plane,** or **air taxi;** Pine Cay has a tiny airstrip that's used by island homeowners and Meridian Club guests. Guests staying 7 nights or more at Pine Cay's Meridian Club enjoy complimentary air-taxi transfers from the Provo airport and boat transfers to and from the island. The Parrot Cay resort arranges taxi and boat transfers for its guests from the Provo airport. A number of the uninhabited cays, such as Fort George Cay and Little Water Cay, are destinations on many local tour-boat operators' half-day and full-day beach excursions.

NORTH CAICOS

At press time, there were no commercial airlines offering flights in and out of the North Caicos airstrip. You can take a ferry from Provo to North Caicos. The **TCI Ferry,** run by Caribbean Cruisin' Ltd. (http://tciferry.com; ℭ **649/946-5406,** cellphone 649/231-4191; $25 single ticket, $40 round-trip adults; $25 round-trip children 9 and under; cash, traveler's checks, and credit cards accepted), offers a ferry service that travels between Provo's Walkin Marina (Heaving Down Rock, Leeward) and North Caicos five times a day from Monday to Saturday and three times on Sunday and holidays; the trip is 25 to 30 minutes long. You can buy your tickets on the ferry. Otherwise, you can get to North Caicos by chartering a water-taxi from one of the many tour-boat operators in the area; it's not cheap, however. Try **Big Blue Unlimited**

 The Causeway Linking North & Middle Caicos

A much-needed causeway linking North and Middle Caicos opened in late 2007, replacing the weekend ferry service between Bottle Creek on North Caicos and Middle Caicos. The 40m (130-ft.) causeway was dedicated to two men, Marco Delroy Williams and Javern Stacey Misick, who died when their boat sank in the creek in January 2007. The causeway was severely damaged during the hurricanes of 2008, and repairs were rudimentary (some say the causeway was poorly engineered to begin with). In places, the causeway blacktop has been completely washed away; you're just bouncing along on limestone rock. Which is to say: It's crossable, but it's slow, rough going. We're talking major potholes and at times little more than a pile of cement blocks separating you from the creek waters. I wouldn't recommend crossing at night, in bad weather, or in a low-riding car. At press time, a major upgrade was rumored to be in the works. Stay tuned.

(www.bigblue.tc; ✆ **649/946-5034;** $300 one-way; boat can accommodate up to eight people); the trip takes around 35 minutes. For ground transportation, call **Gardiner's Taxi** (✆ **649/946-7141**). **Tortoise Taxi & Tours** (✆ **649/241-4778**) will meet you at the North Caicos ferry and give complete tours of North and Middle or tours of Wade's Green or Cottage Pond. Car rentals are highly recommended to fully explore North and Middle; car-rental companies will meet you at the ferry drop-off complete with car, contract, and a local map. Reliable local companies are **Al's Rent-A-Car** (✆ **649/331-1947** or 241-1355), **Old Nick's** (✆ **649/331-8260**), and **Pelican** (✆ **649/946-7139**). Car-rental rates run around $75 a day.

MIDDLE CAICOS

A press time, no commercial airlines were flying between Middle Caicos and Provo, but plans were in the works for regular charter flights out of Provo. You can get to Middle by taking the ferry from Provo to North Caicos (see above) and then renting a car (or hiring a taxi) and driving through North Caicos to Middle. The distance from the Sandy Point ferry to Conch Bar, Middle Caicos, is around 42km (26 miles), a 40-minute drive. Car rentals are highly recommended to fully explore North and Middle; car-rental companies will meet you at the ferry drop-off complete with car, contract, and a local map. Reliable local companies are **Al's Rent-A-Car** (✆ **649/331-1947** or 241-1355), **Old Nick's** (✆ **649/331-8260**), and **Pelican** (✆ **649/946-7139**). Car-rental rates run around $75 a day. *Note:* Be sure to fill up your car with gas in North Caicos; Middle has no gas stations. If you prefer to have someone show you around, Middle Caicos native and guide **Cardinal Arthur** (✆ **649/946-6107;** cellphone 649/241-0730) offers ground transportation, island and cave tours, boat excursions, and fishing expeditions. Cardinal's brother, **Dolphus Arthur** (✆ **649/946-6122**), is one of the island's top fishing guides. Or see Middle Caicos on an eco-tour with **Big Blue Unlimited** (www.bigblue.tc; ✆ **649/946-5034**).

SOUTH CAICOS

Air Turks & Caicos (www.airturksandcaicos.com; ✆ **649/946-4999**) flies daily to South Caicos from Provo; flights cost $120 and take 20 to 25 minutes. Taxis are available at the airport.

GRAND TURK

Most people fly into Providenciales and then take a short flight on a domestic airline into Grand Turk International Airport (also known as J.A.G.S. McCartney International Airport). Several daily flights between Provo and Grand Turk are offered by **Caicos**

Express (www.caicosexpressairways.com; © **649/941-5730**); and **Air Turks & Caicos** (www.airturksandcaicos.com; © **649/946-4999** or 649/946-1667 on Grand Turk). The flight from Provo to Grand Turk takes 30 minutes and costs $140 to $190 round-trip. Caicos Express also flies between Grand Turk and Salt Cay several days a week. It's an easy 8-minute flight, costing around $80 roundtrip.

On Grand Turk you can rent cars (as well as scooters, bicycles, and snorkeling gear) from **Tony's Car Rental** (http://tonyscarrental. com; © **649/964-1879**). Cars and jeeps cost $55 to $100 a day. Scooter rentals cost $60 a day, and bike rentals are $20 a day. You can also rent cars from **Grace Bay Car Rentals** (www.grace baycarrentals.com; © **649/941-8500** or 649/946-4404). Or call Nathan Smith at **Nathan's Golf Cart & Jeep Rentals** (© **649/231-4856**) for jeep and golf cart rentals. Cars and jeeps rent for $70 to $95 a day, scooter rentals cost $40 a day, and bike rentals are $20 a day.

On the days when the cruise ships are in town, **taxis** are few and far between at the Grand Turk airport; it's best to arrange for an airport pickup with your hotel. Keep in mind that most taxi drivers are more than happy to give visitors a tour of the island; expect to pay around $50 to $60 for a 45-minute island tour.

For more information on getting to and getting around Grand Turk, see chapter 5.

SALT CAY

The notoriously tiny airstrip at the Salt Cay airport has been lengthened and resurfaced—but you still need to arrive during daylight hours; the airstrip is not lighted for night. **Caicos Express** (www.caicosexpressairways.com; © **649/941-5730**) offers two flights a day on Monday and Friday and one flight on Wednesday between Salt Cay and Provo. The flight takes 30 minutes and costs $170 roundtrip. Caicos Express also flies between Grand Turk and Salt Cay several days a week. The flight takes 8 minutes and costs around $80 roundtrip.

A government-subsidized **ferry** runs between Grand Turk and Salt Cay, weather permitting, every Tuesday, Wednesday, and Friday (leaving from Deane's Dock—the island's *only* dock, by the way). The trip takes an hour and costs $15 roundtrip (extra charges for luggage). You can also hire a **private boat operator** to take you between Salt Cay and Grand Turk (as long as the seas aren't too rough). The spanking-new *Crystal Seas Adventures* (www.crystal seasadventures.com; © **649/243-9843**) is a spiffy new 27-foot Pro-Cat that can travel between Salt Cay and Grand Turk in 15 minutes, weather permitting (call for rates); it's also a highly recommended operator for dive and snorkel tours. Or hire a boat charter with **Salt Cay Adventure Tours** (http://saltcaytours.com; ✆ 649/946-6909).

No one needs a car to get around Salt Cay, which has more donkeys than cars to begin with; it's the perfect place for getting around on foot, by bike, or by golf cart. Contact **Salt Cay Riders Golf Cart Rentals** (✆ 649/244-1407; two-seater golf carts $65/day, $350/week; credit cards accepted).

For more information on getting to and getting around Salt Cay, see chapter 5.

MONEY & COSTS

CASH/CURRENCY   The U.S. dollar is the legal currency of the Turks and Caicos. Traveler's checks are accepted at most places, as are Visa, MasterCard, and American Express.

ATMS & ABMS   The easiest and best way to get cash away from home is from an ATM. For information on locations and opening times of ATMs (also known as ABMs) on Grand Turk and Salt Cay, see "Fast Facts," p. 148.

Be sure you know your personal identification number (PIN) and your daily withdrawal limit before you leave home. You should also ask your bank about withdrawal fees. Keep in mind that many banks impose a fee every time a card is used at a different bank's ATM, and that that fee is often higher for international transactions than for domestic ones. And if you use a credit card for cash advances, the fees may be higher still—again, check with your bank before you leave home. On top of this, the bank from which you withdraw cash may charge its own fee.

TRAVELER'S CHECKS   Traveler's checks are accepted at most major resorts, but be sure to call to confirm. You can get traveler's

---

   Small Bills & Loose Change

Provo has an increasing number of ATMs (aka ABMs), but don't expect to find a cash machine on every street corner—and the other islands may have only one or two ATMs total (or none, in the case of North and Middle Caicos). So if you plan to travel to some of the less developed islands, it's a good idea to bring plenty of petty cash (small bills and loose change) for snacks, incidentals, and gratuities. Note that the Provo airport is equipped with an ATM: A Scotiabank cash machine is located in the airport check-in hall.

checks at almost any bank. They are offered in denominations of $20, $50, $100, $500, and sometimes $1,000. Generally, you'll pay a service charge ranging from 1% to 4%.

The most popular traveler's checks are offered by **American Express** (© **800/807-6233** or 800/221-7282 for cardholders—this number accepts collect calls, offers service in several foreign languages, and exempts Amex gold and platinum cardholders from the 1% fee), **Visa** (© **800/732-1322**), and **MasterCard** (© **800/223-9920**).

If you carry traveler's checks, be sure to keep a record of their serial numbers separate from your checks in the event that they are stolen or lost. You'll get a refund faster if you know the numbers.

CREDIT CARDS Credit cards are a safe way to carry money, provide a convenient record of all your expenses, and generally offer relatively good exchange rates. You can also withdraw cash advances using a credit card at a bank or ATM, provided you know your PIN. Keep in mind that you'll pay interest from the moment of your withdrawal, even if you pay your monthly bills on time. Also note that many banks now assess a 1% to 3% "transaction fee" on all charges you incur abroad (whether you're using the local currency or your native currency).

Almost every credit card company has an emergency toll-free number that you can call if your wallet or purse is stolen. Credit card companies may be able to wire cash advances immediately, and in many places they can deliver an emergency credit card in a day or two. **Citicorp Visa**'s U.S. emergency number is © **800/336-8472. American Express** cardholders and traveler's check holders should call © **800/221-7282** for all money emergencies. **MasterCard** holders should call © **800/307-7309.**

HEALTH

The Turks and Caicos Islands are great for the soul but may be even better for the body. The TCI has no poisonous snakes or spiders, no malaria or other tropical diseases, and no rabies. The wildest animals you'll find here are the islands' "potcake" dogs (see "Take Home a Potcake . . . or Two," below), which are generally as gentle as lambs. The waters are protected by a coral reef that rings the islands, so big waves and rough, turbulent surf are rare; in fact, the sea is often so gentle and clear (and the sandy bottom so free of rocks) that this is the perfect spot to teach toddlers and young children how to swim.

The exciting news on the TCI health front is the opening of the islands' first modern hospital, the **Turks & Caicos Island Hospital,** in April 2010. It actually comprises two hospitals: the

Cheshire Hall Medical Centre (on Providenciales) and the **Cockburn Town Medical Center** (on Grand Turk).

Keep the following suggestions in mind to stay healthy and safe on your trip:

o **Be mindful of the tropical sun.** Wear sunglasses and a hat and use sunscreen liberally. Limit your time on the beach the first day. If you do overexpose yourself, stay out of the sun until you recover. If your exposure is followed by fever or chills, a headache, or a feeling of nausea or dizziness, see a doctor. And keep hydrated: Drink lots of water if you plan to be outside for long periods.

o **Bring insect repellent.** Fortunately, malaria-carrying mosquitoes in the Caribbean are confined largely to Haiti and the Dominican Republic. But mosquitoes can be a nuisance, especially during the rainy season. In the early evening, the witching hour for skeeters and no-see-'ums, it's a good idea to spray on insect repellent (many restaurants with outdoor seating have insect-repellent spray on hand).

o **Be mindful of diving risks.** The Turks and Caicos is a diver's paradise. One of the more serious risks associated with diving is decompression sickness—more commonly known as "the bends." **Associated Medical Practices** (© **649/946-4242**), located in the Medical Building on Leeward Highway in Providenciales, has a dive decompression chamber to treat the bends. *Note:* The treatment is expensive, so be sure to check your dive insurance before you make the plunge.

o **Consider drinking bottled water during your trip.** If you experience diarrhea, moderate your eating habits and drink only bottled water until you recover. If symptoms persist, consult a doctor.

o **Pack prescription medications in your carry-on luggage.** Carry written prescriptions in generic—not brand-name—form, and dispense all prescription medications from their original labeled vials. Many people try to carry drugs via prescription containers; Customs officials are aware of this type of smuggling and often check medication bottles. (*Exception:* Liquid prescriptions *must* be in their original containers, per the latest Transportation Security Administration regulations.)

o **Pack an extra pair of contact lenses** (if you wear them), in case you lose the first set.

Contact the **International Association for Medical Assistance to Travelers** (**IAMAT;** www.iamat.org; © **716/754-4883,** or 416/652-0137 in Canada) for tips on travel and health concerns on the islands you're visiting and lists of local English-speaking doctors. The **United States' Centers for Disease Control and Prevention** (www.cdc.gov; ✆ **800/CDC-INFO** [232-4636]) provides up-to-date information on health hazards by region or country and offers tips on food safety. The website **www.tripprep. com**, sponsored by a consortium of travel-medicine practitioners, may also offer helpful advice.

What to Do if You Get Sick Away from Home

Finding a good doctor in the Turks and Caicos is not a problem, and most speak English. For contact information on **hospitals, emergency numbers,** and **doctors** and **dentists,** see "Fast Facts," p. 148.

If you suffer from a chronic illness, consult your doctor before your departure. If you worry about getting sick away from home, you might want to consider medical travel insurance.

CRIME & SAFETY

The TCI has long been one of the safest destinations in the Caribbean, but the recession has brought with it something entirely new to these islands: unemployment. And with it has come an uptick in petty crime. Some have attributed the trend to tourism development; others believe the changing population dynamics—the influx of a non-national workforce—is at work, although the global financial downturn and constitutional crisis are certainly factors. The bottom line: Crime is relatively minimal on the islands—the locals, used to a world of unlocked doors, are deeply offended when someone resorts to robbing people of their possessions—but petty theft does take place, so protect your valuables, money, and cameras. Don't flash big wads of money, especially when you arrive at the airport. Use common sense and be aware of your surroundings at all times, and keep your doors locked.

SPECIALIZED TRAVEL RESOURCES

Travelers with Disabilities

Many resorts, condos, and villas in the Turks and Caicos are wheelchair accessible.

Many travel agencies offer customized tours and itineraries for travelers with disabilities. **Flying Wheels Travel** (http://flying wheelstravel.com; ✆ **507/451-5005**) offers escorted tours and cruises that emphasize sports and private tours in minivans with lifts.

TAKE HOME A potcake... OR TWO

The homeless dogs you see roaming the streets of many Caribbean countries generally stay that way: homeless and constantly foraging for food and shelter. The **Turks & Caicos Society for the Prevention of Cruelty to Animals (TCSPCA)** was founded in 2000 to better address the plight of these homeless dogs, here called "potcakes" (the name comes from the food once fed to stray dogs: the caked remains at the bottom of cooking pots). And they've succeeded to a large degree on Provo. You rarely see collarless potcakes running lickety-split along the beach (the Environmental Health department has been cracking down, some say a little too zealously). People who've adopted potcakes report that they're smart, unflappable, incredibly resilient and loving dogs. Potcakes are medium-size dogs and look like the ultimate mutts, with floppy ears and tan or black markings; many a visitor has fallen in love during a stay in the TCI. Along with lobbying the government to adopt animal protection laws and create an animal control unit, the TCSPCA has been instrumental in promoting "off-island adoptions," making it easy for visitors to actually carry home a potcake puppy. Even if you can't adopt, the TCSPCA is always looking for "couriers" to carry puppies on planes to their new homes in the U.S. Every puppy comes with shots and medical certificates and can be carried in the passenger cabins of most airplanes. The big news is the opening of several **Potcake Corners,** stores where you can buy potcake paraphernalia and meet adoptable puppies; you'll find one in the Saltmills Plaza on Grace Bay Road in Provo. For more information, contact the TCSPCA (http://tcspca.tc; © **649/941-8846**) or the island charity set up to improve the lives of TCI potcakes, the **Potcake Foundation** (www.potcakefoundation.com). The **Potcake Place** is a nonprofit rescue organization (www.potcake place.com; © **649/231-1010**).

Access-Able Travel Source (www.access-able.com; © 303/232-2979) offers extensive access information and advice for traveling around the world with disabilities.

Avis Rent a Car has an "Avis Access" program that offers such services as a dedicated 24-hour toll-free number (© 888/879-4273) for customers with special travel needs; special car features such as swivel seats, spinner knobs, and hand controls; and accessible bus service.

Organizations that offer assistance to travelers with disabilities include **MossRehab** (www.mossresourcenet.org), which provides a library of accessible-travel resources online; **SATH** (Society for Accessible Travel & Hospitality; www.sath.org; ✆ 212/447-7284), which offers a wealth of travel resources for all types of disabilities and informed recommendations on destinations, access guides, travel agents, tour operators, vehicle rentals, and companion services; and the **American Foundation for the Blind (AFB;** www.afb.org; ✆ 800/232-5463), a referral resource for the blind or visually impaired that includes information on traveling with Seeing Eye dogs.

Also check out the quarterly magazine *Emerging Horizons* (www.emerginghorizons.com) and *Open World* magazine, published by SATH (see above).

Gay & Lesbian Travelers

Although the TCI is no gay-centric destination, it isn't gay-unfriendly either, especially Provo. I'd call it gay-neutral. The **International Gay and Lesbian Travel Association (IGLTA;** www.iglta.org; ✆ 954/776-2626) is the trade association for the gay and lesbian travel industry, and offers an online directory of gay- and lesbian-friendly travel businesses; go to its website and click on "Members."

Senior Travel

Members of **AARP,** 601 E St. NW, Washington, DC 20049 (www.aarp.org; ✆ 888/687-2277), get discounts on hotels, airfares, and car rentals. AARP offers members a wide range of benefits, including *AARP The Magazine* and a monthly newsletter. Anyone over 50 can join.

Family Travel

The TCI is highly recommended as a family destination. Hotels and resorts by and large welcome families with open arms, and even those with specific adults-only aspects have developed delightful kid-friendly amenities and programs. The gentle, clear, shallow waters and soft-sand beaches of the TCI are particularly attractive for families with toddlers and young children, and older kids will have plenty of nonmotorized watersports activities (snorkeling, sailing, parasailing) to keep them happy. One thing you don't find in the TCI, however, is video-game arcades or similar venues where young teens congregate.

Baby-Equipment Rentals

Most hotels and resorts in Provo are happy to provide cribs, highchairs, and other baby equipment. (Amanyara even provides parents with Diaper Champs, toddler potties, and homemade baby food!) If you're renting a villa or condo, however, you may need to rent baby equipment. **Happy Na** (the owner's name is Naomi) has baby-equipment rentals (cribs, car seats, highchairs, and playpens) as well as baby gifts. They're located at Southwinds Plaza on Leeward Highway in Provo (© **649/941-3568** daytime or 649/941-5326 evenings). Cribs rent for $8 to $20 a day. The shop will deliver equipment 7 days a week from 9am to 8pm.

RESPONSIBLE TOURISM

For the TCI, sustainability of resources is not just a fashionable notion; it's basic survival. For centuries, island inhabitants have had to make do with the resources available to them. The land is largely arid and sandy; rainfall is sparse and fresh water is a scarce and precious commodity.

So far, the government's emphasis on **high-end, low-impact tourism** has worked to temper the impact of rapid development and helped to maintain the delicate balance between commercial interests and environmental ones. Height limits set up for resorts along Grace Bay (famously breached before the recession hit by one high-flying property) have helped stem the potential "New Jersey-ization" of the shoreline. Most of the newer resorts have even implemented their own eco-initiatives. The West Bay Club has its own waste-treatment system and recycles gray water (wastewater from dish, shower, and sink, and laundry water) for landscaping purposes. Each room in the Gansevoort is equipped with an Energy Management System (electricity is turned on with your room key), and a high-efficiency central air-conditioning system reduces energy consumption by 30%.

Of utmost importance to the nation is the maintenance of its most precious natural resource: its pristine **marine environment,** which includes the spectacular **coral reef system.** Maintaining the current status quo is paramount to preventing a "slide towards another spoiled paradise," says Mark Parrish, owner of the watersports operator and eco-pioneer Big Blue Unlimited. "The islands are still beautiful, the seas are still clean, and the reefs are the cornerstone of life," Parrish says. "The future of the TCI must lie in the proper management of the environment and in eco-tourism." Visitors can help out, Parrish suggests, by choosing low-impact excursions.

Eco-tourism got a big boost here when the entire Grace Bay area was awarded **national marine park status.** No commercial or sport fishing is allowed in the protected 2,630-hectare (6,500-acre) Princess Alexandra National Park. This is "no-jet-ski" central, and hopefully never will be. National marine parks have been established on and around just about every island in the TCI; for a full list of protected areas, go to the **Department of Environment and Coastal Services** website at www.environment.tc. Even outside park boundaries, mooring buoys have been established at all dive sites and mooring areas to avoid possible damage from anchors. TCI dive operators are a particularly enlightened bunch with regards to reef preservation and resource conservation.

The scarcity of **fresh water** has always been an issue on these islands—never more so than now with the growing influx of visitors. To prevent water shortages, **modern reverse osmosis plants** have been constructed on Provo and Grand Turk.

GENERAL RESOURCES FOR responsible TRAVEL

The following websites provide valuable wide-ranging information on sustainable travel.

o **Responsible Travel** (www.responsibletravel.com) is a great source of sustainable travel ideas; the site is run by a spokesperson for ethical tourism in the travel industry. **Sustainable Travel International** (www.sustainable travelinternational.org) promotes ethical tourism practices, and manages an extensive directory of sustainable properties and tour operators around the world.

o **Carbonfund** (www.carbonfund.org), **TerraPass** (www. terrapass.org), and **Cool Climate** (http://coolclimate. berkeley.edu) provide info on "carbon offsetting," or offsetting the greenhouse gas emitted during flights.

o **Greenhotels** (www.greenhotels.com) recommends green-rated member hotels around the world that fulfill the company's stringent environmental requirements. **Environmentally Friendly Hotels** (www.environmentally friendlyhotels.com) offers more green accommodation ratings.

The daily air importation of **fresh food** to meet the needs of the tourist population is leaving a hefty carbon footprint, however. It's been estimated that a whopping 90% of food consumed on the islands is imported from the U.S., Haiti, and the Dominican Republic—with a whopping annual price tag to match: The *Turks & Caicos Free Press* reported that in 2008–09 the food import bill came to around $63 million. That's why it's so heartening to hear that agriculture is undergoing a revival in the Turks and Caicos. In the fertile soil of North Caicos—traditionally the breadbasket of the TCI, raising fruits and vegetables for TCI inhabitants throughout the 20th century—farmers are getting a boost from the government. Subsidies are reviving a 58-hectare (143-acre) **Government Organic Farm** in Kew, where demonstration plots are revealing the productive potential of North Caicos soil. The farm grows and sells sweet peppers, hot peppers, tomatoes, callaloo, herbs, okra, squash, and papaya. You can even pay the farm a visit, but be warned: The road is not paved and can be rough and rocky in patches. And retailers are responding to government initiatives. In 2010, Gemma Handy in the *Turks and Caicos Weekly News* reported that the IGA Graceway supermarket in Provo was buying up spectacular okra grown by septuagenarian farmer Emanuel Misick on his 8.1-hectare (20-acre) Green Acre Farm in Bottle Creek.

STAYING CONNECTED
Without Your Own Computer

Many **hotels** and **resorts** in the TCI feature "libraries" or small business centers where guests have complimentary use of computers with high-speed Internet access. The number of computers available is often limited, however, and you may have to wait your turn to use one.

With Your Own Computer

The wireless world is up and rolling in the Turks and Caicos; most resorts have wireless Internet access. For dial-up access, most business-class hotels offer dataports for laptop modems. In addition, major Internet service providers (ISPs) have **local access numbers** around the world, allowing you to go online by placing a local call. The **iPass** network also has dial-up numbers around the world. You'll have to sign up with an iPass provider, who will then tell you how to set up your computer for your destination(s). For a list of iPass providers, go to www.ipass.com and click on "Individuals Buy Now." One solid provider is **i2roam** (www.i2roam.com; ⓒ **866/811-6209** or 920/235-0475).

calling **HOME**

Making international calls from the Turks and Caicos can be costly, in particular if you're dialing direct from your hotel room, when you'll be charged more than $2 a minute. You cannot access most U.S. toll-free numbers from the TCI; for example, you won't be able to use AT&T prepaid calling cards here. You can use any GSM cellphone if it has international roaming capabilities. One way to avoid the high costs of calling home from your hotel room is to **buy a prepaid cellphone** in the TCI. You can purchase a cellphone for as low as $60; it comes with a $10 phone card. Additional prepaid phone cards come in $10, $20, $50, and $75 denominations. Phones and cards can be found at the **LIME** offices on Leeward Highway ((𝄞 **649/946-2200**) and at the Graceway IGA Supermarket (LIME has a small office at the entrance). Another option is to **rent a cellphone.** Many hotels and resorts offer cellphone rentals ($10/day; $30/week), as do Grant's Texaco Downtown and Kathleen's 7-Eleven on Leeward Highway. Another easy option is to buy a magicJack (www.magic jack.com). Simply plug the headset or phone into your computer, dial the number, and talk for free.

GETTING MARRIED IN THE TURKS & CAICOS

Turks & Caicos is a hot destination-wedding spot, as TCI's former premier, the Honorable Dr. Michael Misick, proved when he married Hollywood starlet LisaRaye McCoy (star of the UPN comedy *All of Us*) in 2006 in a celebrity-studded wedding at Amanyara. (It's no guarantee that the marriage will last, alas; theirs didn't.) You can get married barefoot on the beach, in a ballroom at a luxury resort, on a sailboat, or in one of the island's colorful churches, to name a few choice scenarios. An increasing number of resorts and tour operators are equipped to handle weddings soup-to-nuts. Here is a sampling of options:

o **Sail Provo** (www.sailprovo.com) can organize a wedding on one of its large catamarans or on a secluded beach, with all the trimmings, for up to 100 people.

o The **Regent Palms** resort offers customized wedding services and your choice of ceremony locations (on the beach; in the Palms Court, which was featured in the Aug 2005 issue of *Modern Bride*; or in the Messel Ballroom) and reception locations (in the Messel Ballroom, on the beachside wooden deck, or in the courtyard).

- **Beaches Turks & Caicos** (© 800/SANDALS [726-3257]) marries couples on a regular basis—in high season as many as *80 couples a month.* It's big business for Beaches, and they take it very seriously, with an on-site wedding coordinator and complete wedding packages to choose from.

You need to meet the following legal requirements to marry in the TCI: You will need to bring a passport, a copy of your birth certificate, proof of status from your place of residence (if single, a sworn affidavit), and a divorce decree if you're divorced. You will need to pay a $50 license fee. You must be on island for 72 hours to establish residency, and the marriage license takes 2 to 3 days to process. *Note:* If you plan to marry in one of the island churches, you may need proof of membership.

The Turks and Caicos Islands marriage certificate is legally recognized in the U.S., Canada, and the U.K. For more details, contact the **Registry of Births, Deaths and Marriages** on Front Street at © **649/946-2800** in Grand Turk (the Registry also has an office in Provo at © **649/946-5350**).

TIPS ON ACCOMMODATIONS

HOTELS & RESORTS Many budget travelers assume they can't afford the big hotels and resorts. But there are so many packages out there and so many advertised sales during the off season that you might be pleasantly surprised at what you can get. In addition, many hotels offer upgrades whenever they have a big block of rooms to fill and few reservations.

Most of the resorts along Provo's Grace Bay are condo hotels. These properties are nothing more than hotels whose units are sold to individual owners or investors, usually even before the hotel is built. Most units then enter the resort "rental pool" when the owner is not using the unit.

ALL-INCLUSIVE RESORTS The ideal all-inclusive is just that— a place where *everything*—meals, drinks, and most watersports—is included. In the Turks and Caicos, three resorts now bill themselves as all-inclusive: **Beaches, Club Med Turkoise,** and the **Veranda.** The all-inclusive market is geared to the active traveler who likes organized entertainment, lots of sports and workouts at fitness centers, and plenty of food and drink—and all three resorts come through in these categories.

In the 1990s, so many competitors entered the all-inclusive market that the term means different things to the different resorts that embrace this marketing strategy. With the TCI all-inclusives, all meals, drinks, and gratuities are included, for example, but you'll have to pay for extras such as certain spa treatments or optional scuba-diving services. At the island's newest all-inclusive, the Veranda, menu items have prices attached—a neat bit of transparency that lets you know exactly what you're paying for, but that can have the opposite effect of making you think those items cost extra to order.

The all-inclusives have a reputation for being expensive, but to many people, not having to "pay as you go" or deal with gratuities is liberating and worth the money. If you're looking for ways to cut costs with an all-inclusive, the trick is to travel in off-peak periods, which doesn't always mean just from mid-April to mid-December. If you want a winter vacation at an all-inclusive, choose the month of January—not February or the Christmas holidays, when prices are at their all-year high. The resorts also regularly offer special packages for weeklong stays; check hotel websites for the latest offerings.

GUESTHOUSES/INNS An entirely different type of accommodations is the guesthouse. In the Caribbean the term "guesthouse" can mean any number of things. Some so-called guesthouses are more or less simple motels built around swimming pools. Others are small individual cottages with their own kitchenettes, constructed around a main building in which you'll often find a bar and a restaurant that serves local food. Still others are small, owner-operated inns of five rooms or less that come with private bathrooms, fine linens, and boutique amenities. The guesthouse or inn usually represents excellent value, simply because it does not have the full-service amenities of a resort or hotel.

In the TCI, you can find inns or guesthouses on Grand Turk, Salt Cay, North Caicos, Middle Caicos, and South Caicos.

RENTING A VILLA, CONDO, OR HOUSE A "housekeeping holiday" can be one of the least expensive ways to vacation in the Turks and Caicos, especially if you're traveling with a large group of family members or friends. Plus, it's a good way to go if you prefer your vacations with a modicum of privacy and independence. Most villas, condos, and private homes include fresh linens and towels, fully equipped kitchens, TV/DVDs, washer/dryers, and beach chairs. Some come with regular maid service and even personal chefs.

In the simpler villa or house rentals, doing your own cooking and laundry or even your own maid service may not be your idea of a good time in the sun. But you'll save money, especially for a family of three to six people, or a group of two or three couples—up to 50% to 60% of what you would pay to stay in a hotel. Even though groceries are sometimes priced 35% to 60% higher than on the

U.S. mainland (import duties are astronomical), preparing your own food is a lot cheaper than dining at restaurants.

Of course, you *can* spend a lot of money renting a house or villa in the TCI, which has no dearth of seriously lavish homes for rent in prime beachfront settings. Many come complete with the services of a staff and a personal chef.

Multi-unit condos are often comparable to a suite in a big resort hotel. Condo complexes often have reception desks, pools (some more than one), and fully equipped kitchens but little else in the way of hotel amenities. Like villas, condos range widely in price.

Keep in mind that not all house, villa, and condo rentals come complete with everything you need for a TCI vacation. You may have to rent watersports equipment, for example, or baby cribs.

For a list of agencies that arrange rentals in Providenciales, see the few recommended options below. If you're looking for rentals in North or Middle Caicos, check out the properties on the **Turks & Caicos Tourist Board** website (www.turksandcaicostourism. com). For villa and house rentals in Grand Turk and Salt Cay, see chapter 5.

Make your reservations well in advance. Here are a few agencies that rent villas in Provo and elsewhere:

- **Tranquility** (www.turkscaicosluxuryvillas.com; © 649/431-1474) handles a number of unique private properties, including some beautiful villas directly on Grace Bay Beach near the Beaches resort.
- **Turks & Caicos Reservations** (www.turksandcaicos reservations.tc; © 877/774-5486) is a wealth of island information. The company handles over a hundred villas and offers resort/hotel packages as well.
- **North Shore Villas** (www.northshorevillas.com; © 404/467-4858) has a number of deluxe free-standing private villas, most of which are located on Grace Bay Beach, as well as other vacation villa properties all over Provo.
- **Prestigious Properties** (http://prestigiousproperties.com; © 649/946-4379) offers a range of villas, condos, and single-family residences.
- **Seafeathers Villas** (www.seafeathers.com; © 649/941-5703) has a variety of beachfront villas, cottages, and condos, many with private pools and oceanfront locations. Chefs, maids, and babysitters are also available on request.
- **Ocean Point Villas** (www.oceanpointvillas.com; © 404/467-4858) has lovely deluxe villas ranging in size from two to seven bedrooms in the strictly residential neighborhood of Ocean Point and on the North Shore near Turtle Cove.

[FastFACTS] TURKS & CAICOS

Area Code   The area/country code for the TCI is **649**.

ATMs & ABMs   **Scotiabank** (www.scotiabank.com; ℭ **649/946-4750**) has 24-hour ATMs (serving both Cirrus and PLUS networks) at Waterloo Plaza on Grand Turk and at four locations on Provo: at the Provo airport check-in hall; at the Graceway Gourmet on Grace Bay Road; next to the Graceway IGA on Leeward Highway; and at Petro Plus on Millennium Highway. **FirstCaribbean International Bank** (www.firstcaribbeanbank.com; ℭ **649/946-4245**) has 24-hour ABM (PLUS network) service at its main branches on Provo, Grand Turk, and South Caicos and a branch in the Saltmills shopping complex on Provo's Grace Bay Road. The **Royal Bank of Canada (RBC)** has a 24-hour ABM at its Centre Mews Branch on Leeward Highway in Providenciales (www.rbcroyalbank.com; ℭ **649/941-4776**).

Banks   Branches and ATMs of **FirstCaribbean** and **Scotiabank** are at convenient and central locations on both Provo and Grand Turk (see "ATMs & ABMs," above).

Business Hours   Banks are generally open Monday to Thursday from 8:30am to 2:30pm and Friday from 8:30am to 4:30pm. Most stores are open daily from 10am to 6pm, but hours vary. Many stores on Grand Turk close for lunch. Most grocery stores are open 7 days a week but do not sell liquor, beer, or wine on Sunday. Many businesses keep limited hours in the off season or close altogether.

Currency   The **U.S. dollar** is the official currency.

Dentists   **Dental Services Limited** is located in the Medical Building on Leeward Highway in Providenciales (www.dentist.tc; ℭ **649/946-4321**).

Doctors   **Dr. Sam Slattery** sees patients at the **Grace Bay Medical Centre,** offering both interisland medical services and urgent care (Neptune Plaza, Allegro Rd., Providenciales; ℭ **649/941-5252;** emergencies: 649/231-0525). **Associated Medical Practices** is located in the Medical Building on Leeward Highway in Providenciales (www.doctor.tc; ℭ **649/946-4242;** emergencies: 649/331-4357). Associated also has a dive recompression chamber.

Drugstores   There are three full-service pharmacies: **Grace Bay Pharmacy,** located in Neptune Plaza on Dolphin Drive between Grace Bay Road and the Leeward Highway (ℭ **649/946-8242**); **Island Pharmacy,** in the Associated Medical Building on Leeward Highway in Providenciales (ℭ **649/946-4150**); and **Flamingo Pharmacy,** in the Cabot House, the IGA Graceway Complex (www.flamingo pharmacy.com; ℭ **649/941-4527**).

Electricity The electric current on the islands is 120 volts, 60 cycles, AC. European appliances will need adapters.

Emergencies Call ℂ **911** or **999** for an **ambulance,** to report a **fire,** or to contact the **police.**

Hospitals & Medical Facilities **Turks & Caicos Island Hospital** has two centers: the **Cheshire Hall Medical Centre,** Hospital Rd., Providenciales (ℂ **649/941-2800**) and the **Cockburn Town Medical Center,** Hospital Rd., Grand Turk (ℂ **649/941-2900**), both staffed and operated by InterHealth Canada. **Grace Bay Medical Centre,** Neptune Plaza, Allegro Road, is an urgent-care medical facility on Providenciales (ℂ **649/941-5252;** for emergencies call ℂ **649/231-0525**). **Grand Turk Hospital** is on Hospital Road on Grand Turk (ℂ **649/946-2040**). The other islands have community clinics.

Internet Access Most resorts and hotels offer Wi-Fi Internet access, but keep in mind that service can be slow and spotty on the less-developed islands.

Language The official language is English.

Pets Visitors wishing to bring a pet onto the islands need an import permit ($50), 48 hours' notice of arrival, and a signed veterinary health certificate (dated within 1 month of travel) stating that the animal is free of contagious or infectious disease and up-to-date on his or her rabies and distemper vaccinations. For specifics, contact the **TCI Environmental Health Department** at ℂ **649/946-2801.** There is no quarantine period for incoming pets.

Post Office The Provo Post Office and Philatelic Bureau is located downtown at the corner of Airport Road. It's open Monday to Thursday from 8am to 4pm and Friday from 8am to 3:30pm. The Grand Turk Post Office is located on Front Street in Cockburn Town. It's open Monday to Friday from 8am to 4pm.

Taxes There is a departure tax of $35, payable when you leave the islands (it's often included in the cost of your airfare). The government collects an 11% occupancy tax, applicable to all hotels, guesthouses, and restaurants in the 40-island chain. Many resorts charge an additional 10% service or resort tax on top of the government tax.

Note: In November 2011, the interim government announced a 20% tax hike on alcohol and tobacco, a "sin tax" that, coupled with a new 20% import duty on alcohol and gasoline, all but guaranteed steep price hikes for alcoholic beverages throughout the islands.

Telephone To call the Turks and Caicos, dial **1** and then the number. The country code for the TCI is **649.** The international-operator telephone service is ℂ **115.** Local directory assistance is ℂ **118.**

To call a phone carrier in the U.S., dial **0,** then **1,** and then the number. You can make domestic and international calls using your credit card or prepaid phone cards, available in $5, $10, and $15 denominations—although rates for either are often as exorbitant as they are if you call direct from your hotel room ($2 a minute, depending on the time of day—many hotels even charge $1 and up for local calls). Public pay phones accept prepaid phone cards only. You can buy these prepaid phone cards at a number of retail outlets and hotels. If you have a GSM cellphone with international roaming capacity, you can use that on the islands; a money-saving option is to buy or rent a cellphone in the TCI (see "Calling Home," earlier in this chapter).

Time The islands are in the Eastern Standard Time zone, and daylight saving time is observed.

Tipping Hotels often add 10% to 15% to your bill automatically, a "resort fee" to cover service. If individual staff members perform various services for you, it is customary to tip them something extra. If you go on an island tour, watersports charter, or beach excursion, it's always a good idea to tip your guide 10% to 20%, depending on the level of service you receive. In restaurants 15% is appropriate unless a service charge has already been added; if in doubt, ask. Tip taxi drivers 10% to 15%.

Vaccinations No vaccinations are required for travelers to the TCI.

Visas No visas are required for travelers staying up to 30 days. For more information, go to www.immigrationboard.tc.

Water Government officials say that the water in the Turks and Caicos is safe to drink. Nonetheless, you may want to stick to bottled water, especially if you have a delicate stomach.

Index

See also Accommodations and Restaurant indexes, below.

General Index

Accommodations

Restaurants